HOW TO LIVE WITH A CAT

by

Margaret Cooper Gay

MEDICAL REVISIONS BY J. R. STERLING, D.V.M.

Line drawings by Roberta MacDonald

Medical illustrations by Judith Ann Lawrence

A FIRESIDE BOOK

Published by Simon and Schuster

A Fireside Book
Published by Simon and Schuster
Rockefeller Center, 630 Fifth Avenue
New York, New York 10020

First paperback printing 1971
SBN 671-20199-9 Casebound edition
SBN 671-20912-4 Fireside paperback edition
Manufactured in the United States of America

TO

MARY PRITCHETT

WHO HAS BEEN A FRIEND IN DEED

Foreword

How to Live with a Cat *is, in my opinion, a sound and helpful manual. It completely covers what we need to know in order to meet any situation or emergency encountered by the family cat. It should be particularly useful to the new cat owner—and we can all learn new things from it. I, for one, was surprised to learn that tyrants have always hated cats, and many other bits of lore and legend here were new to me. If you read this book only for the story of the author's own three cats, you will enjoy knowing them, and you will learn how to care for a cat in the city or in the country, for these three are cats of wide experience. Whether you want to know how to help a cat raise kittens, or what to do when the cat jumps on a hot stove and burns its feet, or how to estimate your cat's I.Q., the information is here.*

NORMAN H. JOHNSON, D.V.M.

Author's Note

IN REVISING this book I have tried to answer all the sensible questions that have been asked, and to provide the latest information on the care of cats. The theory of feeding cats has changed considerably and, it seems, for the better. There's plenty of good flea powder about, if you know how the label should read. Most important of all, veterinary medicine has advanced a hundred years in the last seven. Diseases which were considered incurable can now often be routed in days, thanks to antibiotics and the other new medicines. Operations that were "impossible" are becoming routine successes in the best veterinary hospitals. The science of geriatrics has even been applied to aging cats so they live longer and are happier. In short, the time has gone by when a nice person with good intentions could tell others what to do for sick cats. The information about antibiotics, antihistamines and the rest of the wonderful new medicines for cats contained in the chapter on "Accidents and Ailments" has been written in collaboration with Norman H. Johnson, D.V.M., Head Clinician of the New York City Hospital of the American Society for the Prevention of Cruelty to Animals, and J. R. Sterling, D.V.M.

MARGARET COOPER GAY

Contents

Food for the working cat ... What to feed a cat
(Fats and oils, Insides, Muscle meat, Eggs, Fish,
Poultry and game, Prepared foods, Pâtés de la
maison, Bones, Vegetables, Table scraps, Liquid
refreshment) *... Temperature ... How much
food? ... How often? ... Dietary don'ts ... If
the cat won't eat.*

Six weeks to three months (Six meals a day) *...
Three to four months* (Five meals a day) *...
Four to five months* (Four meals a day) *...
Five to six months* (Three meals a day).

*Foster mothers ... What to do if you can't get a
foster mother* (Are you that anxious to raise kittens?) *... The kittens' box ... Warmth ... Food
... The kittens' eyes ... The first meat ...
Weaning.*

*A cat's destiny ... Planned kittens ... Cats that
should not be bred ... The cat's choice ... Feeding the pregnant cat ... What to do when the kittens are born ... How to destroy unwanted kittens
... Care of the mother cat after her kittens have
been killed ... How to feed a nursing cat ...
When to start feeding the kittens.*

Who Keeps Cats and Why

Nobody knows how many cats there are in the United States. Various organizations and individuals have estimated that there are fifteen million, fifty million, a hundred and fifty million cats, which proves only that there are a lot of cats. Certainly for every dog that has a home at least three cats share food and fireside, which gives us about fifty million cats to begin with. Then there are the free-lance cats that go their own way, earn their own living, and ask no odds of any man. Since all cats are potential alley cats, and any alley cat is potentially a pampered pet, their status shifts from day to day and one man's census is as good as another's. Additional millions of cats earn their living on docks and piers and ships, in public buildings, offices and warehouses, in shops and factories and barns, without having homes in the conventional sense of the word. Career cats are quite well off so they will be mentioned with respectful restraint in these pages which are addressed to people who live with cats, would like to live with cats, or might be converted to the idea of living with cats.

Cats are charming companions, good friends and a lot of fun, which you'd think would be reason enough for living with them, but some people need solider reasons. They never stop reminding themselves that they are "reasoning human beings," and a lot of them insist on having reasons for doing such pleasant things as eating cake or living with cats. Unless they can say with mock-rueful smugness, "It's a terrible vice and I really must stop," they won't admit doing anything just because it's fun. One man I know says his friends own dogs to flatter their egos, and that he lives with cats to keep his ego humble. Another finds cats aloof, incomprehensible and therefore fascinating; he firmly believes they hold the key to occult mysteries. I know a woman who lives with cats because "they're such innocent little dears." And so it goes.

Some people keep cats only to catch mice and rats, which is a worthy reason and probably satisfies the cats. If more people did the same we wouldn't have a rat problem. There are people who keep and breed cats in the hope of making money from them, which is a reason, though growing potatoes might pay better.

The solitary introvert lives with a cat because he's lonely and won't admit it; and a cat is the only creature with dignity and self-respect enough to live with him and love him and mind its own business.

The exuberant extrovert is always bringing home a playful kitten and then feeling abused when it grows up to be a cat;

The solitary introvert lives with a cat

and the cat feels hard-done-by because anybody ought to know that nature takes its course. Usually, however, they settle their differences and become good friends, especially if the cat keeps the house stocked with kittens.

Artists and writers, creative people of all sorts, even news-papermen who sometimes graduate into the creative class, like cats. This, I think, is because such people must be free or perish, and cats feel the same way. Nobody can tell an author how to write a book or a cat how to catch a mouse. Swinburne, Victor Hugo, Baudelaire, Tasso, Rostand, and Mark Twain were among the literary cat lovers of other days. In our own time Louis Untermeyer, Ernest Hemingway, Paul Gallico, Elmer Davis, James Mason and Pamela Kellino are outspoken friends of cats.

There's a natural affinity between statesmen and cats. Both know what they want and find ways to get it. Mazarin, Riche-lieu, Chateaubriand, Colbert, and Wolsey loved cats. They must have liked the grace and dignity of cats, their aloofness to mortal strife, and their superlative concentration on the business of beings cats. They must also have admired the diplomacy of cats, straightforward, resourceful, and indomitable beyond the imagination of human schemers.

Mohammed so loved cats that he cut off the hem of his robe rather than disturb Muessa, his favorite. He decreed punishment for abusing cats, and to this day a Mohammedan's house is home only if a cat lives there.

Martin Luther and Lenin were devoted to cats. Superficially this seems illogical because they were both reformers, and nobody ever heard of a cat that wanted to make everybody eat mice. The explanation is that before they became reformers, Luther and Lenin were rebels, and rebels always have been in-

Even newspapermen like cats

dependent souls. Cats and rebels go together like bread and butter.

People who love freedom love cats. Thomas Jefferson, George Washington, and Abraham Lincoln loved liberty and cats. Winston Churchill's close friend was a big black cat named Nelson.

Tyrants hate cats. Alexander the Great, Julius Caesar, Genghis Khan, Napoleon I, and Mussolini head the list, which includes any bully you can think of. I haven't been able to find out how Hitler felt about cats; I'll bet you a cookie he hated them. All the little fuehrers I ever met were cat haters, and I don't know a single cat hater who isn't also a dictator at heart —if dictators have hearts. A bully simply can't endure living with anything he can't boss, and nobody can boss a cat.

In general men understand cats better than women do. Independence is more a part of man-nature than of woman-nature, and men who aren't specially independent characters themselves respect independence when they meet it. The trouble is that few men are independent enough to admit liking cats. Most of them are henpecked by the cat haters and cowed by hunters who begrudge a cat a rabbit, so they look sheepish and act bashful whenever cats are mentioned. If they had the gumption of a sick cat they'd tell the ailurophobes and the mighty hunters to go climb a tree.

Women talk a lot about loving cats and are talked about for it even more. A lot of women do love cats, and very few indeed hate them. Some women understand cats. Others like cats because they're soft and cuddlesome, and cats like to be cuddled—nothing is so affectionate as a cat with cold feet— which pleases all concerned, though there's a lot more to living with a cat than warming its feet.

Living with a cat is like being married to a career woman who can take domesticity or let it alone, so you'd better be nice to her. I have known cats that left cream and cushions and cuddling for the hard liberty of alleys.

The fact that cats can live with us or leave us is grist for the mills of the cat haters, who seize on every example of feline independence to shout that cats are unfaithful and unloving. Some cats are, and so are some people. Other cats shame us by their devotion. Cats actually have brought food to starving, helpless people. We can all be sure our cats live with us because they love us; otherwise they'd leave.

People who pay out money for physical possession of cats do not thereby become cat owners. Nobody owns a cat. A person can be a humane jailer or a cat's best friend. If anywhere in these pages I refer to any of the cats who share my home as "my cat, Ma," or "my cat, Charlie," the term is used exactly as if I said, "my friend, Mary."

One of the most delightful aspects of living with a cat is the cat's serene conviction of equality, with the absence of any trace of master-and-slave relationship. I take care of my cats because I like their company. They live with me because they like my company, and they pay board by keeping my house free of rodents, my garden free of snakes, and my heart young.

Ma, whom I call "the Missus" behind her back, is the boss cat at my house, though I alone in all this world hold her dear. The Missus would drive a poet mad, she'd give a banker nervous prostration, and I daren't think what she'd do to an artist.

She's an out-of-shape old trollop, tortoise-shell and white, with a rowdy black patch over one eye, a yellow smudge on her lip, and a beautiful strong head under the variegated patches. She walks with a three-way swagger, her middle swinging east and west like an overloaded hammock when she goes north. She is at once complacent and bellicose, with an air of knowing the answer to any problem.

The Missus used to be a wild cat. I saw her often in the woods that winter, staring from behind a tree, vanishing at a word like a pied ghost cat. Then one spring morning she gave up. Starved, tottering, her neck slashed by dog bites, Ma crept to my back door and meekly asked for a handout. I fed her, stroked and pitied her, and she wasn't wild any more. She led me to a hollow tree far back in the woods where four newborn kittens were crying feebly for milk she was too starved to make for them. I had five cats then.

In no time at all Ma's meekness vanished. She got fat, and her pride in that pot belly which wasn't kittens surpassed the pride of a butcher's wife at the Court of St. James'. (She still likes to roll and show what a rich cat she is.) She sits in the best chairs and the softest laps. She won't go out when the weather is bad, and when I put her out she tells the neighbors her folks don't treat her right. She is devoted to children, even rough ones, and she's as scared of bugs as my grandmother was of mice.

I don't know how old the Missus is. Although she's had beaux in three states and a half dozen neighborhoods, the kittens born in the hollow tree were her last. She's deaf and farsighted and doesn't catch mice any more. She's useless, cantankerous, raucous, and homely. She's also valiant and loyal and kind.

Ma's son, Picklepuss, also known as Monsieur du Piquel, His Pickleship, and Dammit, lives with me too. Pickle is a big red and white altered cat, with a long, doggy face and a scientific turn of mind. As a hunter, Pickle specializes in snakes. He'll fight any strange cat at the drop of a whisker, and the dog doesn't live that can make him back up, which may some day be Pickle's undoing.

Pickle is deliberate and thorough in all things. One rainy

morning he saw a big black cat in his yard. He whined and I let him out. He chased the cat two fences down, came in, shook the rain off, and sat down to wash. After a few licks he stopped, went out again, and chased the cat halfway down the block. He came home, shook himself, and again settled into the position of a cat about to wash. He paused with one hind leg straight up, gazed at the door a while, sneezed, and went out a third time. The sounds of battle were shrill and loud and long. Pickle finally came home, soaking wet, shook water all over the house, and washed from A to Izzard without looking up. I never saw that black cat again.

Pickle co-operates with Ma and Charlie in routing any common enemy. The rest of the time he prefers the company of people and lets cats know it. He loves his own people to distraction and will even endure discomfort to be near us. In his dealings with the rest of the world Pickle is a total snob—you'd never guess he was born in a hollow tree. My cat-hating acquaintances abhor him beyond all other cats; which is funny, for Pickle has the making of a first-rate ailurophobe himself.

He'd be a good cat for a cardinal or a king. Sometimes I wonder what he sees in me.

Charlie, my third cat, is a foundling, half puss, half pixie, and wholly charming. Charlie is tall and slim and blue all over, silvery gray with a violet sheen, and he is grace itself. Even ailurophobes admit that he is lovely.

Charlie is a glamour puss. Our feminine neighbors brush and comb him, tie dangerous ribbons and bells to his collar. Once he came home wearing a tag that had a girl's telephone number on it. Several of the girls have asked for Charlie's hand, and it takes the whole family, including Charlie, to make each one understand that she is only a passing fancy and not the love of Charlie's life.

Charlie accepts all this attention and goes his way, serene, inscrutable and a little wistful—except at dinner time, when he's an outright glutton. He is loving and gentle at home. Strangers can't touch him. I imagine the cat-gods of Egypt must have resembled Charlie. Poets and painters delight in him. He probably was intended to keep a saint or a sorcerer company. I don't understand Charlie and expect I never shall, though we love each other very much.

Ben, on the other hand, is a cat anybody with reasonable intelligence can understand. Ben is Ma's son and Pickle's brother. When Ben was a kitten I gave him to friends who needed a cat. He has more than filled their need; he's visiting cat for the whole block.

When one of the neighbors has the Garden Club in for tea, Ben is there to greet the guests, show the garden, and lead the way to the refreshments, knowing special liver canapés have been set aside for him. His presence lends dignity and tone to cocktail parties, dinners, and weddings—any occasion, in short, which calls for fancy vittles. Ben comforts the sick and shares their milk, persuades the sorrowful to cheer up and open a can of sardines.

Ben does not steal food. On the other hand, it is hard to imagine how Ben could get hungry.

Ben catches mice at home, and he brings in the neighbors' mice, sometimes with trap attached. One summer Ben took a fancy to a neighbor's pet frog, brought it home every night, undamaged, and turned it loose to leap moistly in and out of people's beds.

Ben receives Christmas cards and even letters from friends in far places. Once the Consolidated Edison Company wrote him a letter, addressed to Benjamin K. Britton, Esq., no less! requesting a ten dollar deposit on his gas and electric meters. Ben's people had a lovely time answering that one.

Ben lives with a dog so little and excitable that it can be played with only from a distance, and then gingerly. This Ben does with extraordinary restraint.

In the bosom of his family Ben is a cat of suave dignity and sophisticated charm. Only a twinkle in his eye hints of cocktail parties and frog-nappings and cat-about-town gallivantings.

There's a cat for anyone sensible, tolerant, wise, and kind enough to live with a cat successfully. There are stodgy cats for stodgy people, businesslike cats for practical people, beautiful cats for artistic souls. There are smart cats, wise cats, stupid, sly, and indifferent cats, feline rascals and feline geniuses to fit the proper people. You need only to discover a cat, or be discovered by one, which suits you and which you suit.

II

A Cat's-eye View of History

If cats wrote history books they'd be fairer to us, I think, than human historians are to cats. We grudgingly admit that cats catch mice, but refuse to consider what a world this would be if they didn't. Surely cats would allow that we invented the comforts which their diligence helps them and us to enjoy. Since cats are not historians, I have compiled on their behalf this brief sketch of the relations between cats and men since first we took up with each other.

In the beginning people were tramps. They wandered around picking berries and throwing rocks at rabbits. People were careless with bones, when they had any bones, and so dogs followed them. When a dog caught a rabbit and boastfully brought it home, the people took most of the rabbit in payment for last week's bone. Sometimes the dogs helped to run down wild sheep and cattle and then there were plenty of hand-me-down bones. When times were bad the people ate roast puppy. When enemies attacked, the dogs barked a warning and helped defend their homes. This enabled people to live a little better than dogs, so they called the dog Man's Best Friend.

Then, somewhere in Egypt, cats found out that people drew mice. Cats didn't swap freedom for a gnawed bone, as dogs did. Cats took up with people to get a bargain in mice, but they have kept their liberty to this day. People soon learned that they had the best of the bargain. Thanks to cats, they could raise a crop and store the grain and have enough to eat all winter long— something that never had happened before.

People in Egypt grew tall and strong and wise. They built the pyramids to serve as clocks, calendars, and planting charts to all the inhabitants of the valley of the Nile. They mastered the arts and sciences, perfected astronomy and geometry, and made the cat a god. They made the rat a god too—a dual god, the god of judgment because it always nibbled the freshest loaf, and the god of utter destruction because what it did not eat it fouled.

The Egyptians called the cat Mau, which was, and is, the cat's own name for itself.

It is said that Egyptians took cats hunting in packs, like foxhounds. This probably was to give the cats an outing, rather than to get them an extra rabbit, for fish were kept in special tanks to feed the cats.

According to Herodotus, Egyptian law required a man to shave his eyebrows as a sign of mourning when the cat died. Killing a cat was a crime punishable by death.

The exportation of cats was forbidden, and Egyptian soldiers in foreign lands were required to catch all the cats they saw and send them home.

This last law was aimed at the Greeks, who for centuries had been chiseling a knowledge of geometry, astronomy, philosophy, and the arts from Egypt, and had realized at last that they needed cats. The Greeks had tried encouraging weasels to live around the house and catch mice, but weasels didn't particularly care for mice; they were just killing-fools. Birds, poultry, eggs, hares, anything short of a goat, was weasel-bait. Also, weasels were unfriendly, sly, and smelly. Greeks who didn't like weasels laid sprigs of alder or mullein around their grain boxes and planted asphodel about the barn in the hope of discouraging mice—they still had mice. Since the Egyptians had a corner on cats, the only way a Greek could get a cat was to steal it. They sent spies to Egypt to steal cats, and the Egyptians sent their spies to Greece to steal the cats back. Cat-stealing and counter-cat-stealing went on for several hundred years. Finally Greece grew great on chiseled knowledge and stolen cats.

With cats enough to insure a well-stocked granary, the population multiplied until Greece was downright crowded, and the wars of conquest began that ruined both Greece and Egypt. Alexander the Great was a cat hater, as nearly all conquerors have been, and in 332 B.C. he conquered Egypt, possibly with the idea of eliminating cats. The conquest didn't stick, so cats were not eliminated.

The war that ended Egypt's greatness was started by a cat. A Roman who lived in Egypt accidentally killed a cat. The enraged Egyptians killed the Roman. At the end of a long war Mark Antony killed himself, the asp bit Cleopatra, Egypt became a Roman province, and the cat ceased to be a god in the valley of the Nile.

At this point it is customary to say that the cat, no longer a god, became an outcast and the companion of witches. That may be good literature. It isn't history. The cat was the symbol of liberty throughout the great days of Greece and Rome. The

Roman goddess of liberty was represented with a cup in one
hand, a broken scepter in the other, and a cat at her feet. Later
the cat became the symbol of liberty in Switzerland. Even today
the cat is sacred to Mohammedans and Hindus, and is the only
animal so honored by both. Feeding the cat at dinner is part of
the orthodox Hindu rite.

Cats reached Persia in the Fifth or Sixth Century A.D., and
by the year 1000 they had traveled to China and Japan, where
they were a highly valued curiosity.

On the nineteenth day of the ninth month of the year 999
a cat had young in the Imperial Palace of the Emperor of Japan.
The Emperor ordered his Ministers of the Right and the Left
to rear the kittens. A court lady was appointed as nurse, and
when the kittens grew up they were kept on leashes. This,
naturally, prevented the cats from catching mice. The Japanese apparently thought cats served as a charm to keep mice
away, and people who couldn't afford cats set up statues or
paintings of cats to scare the mice, as we put scarecrows in
cornfields. (Oddly, they still think a statue or a painting is
pretty near as good as a cat—even the silkworm breeders who
are terrorized by rats.) It wasn't until 1602 that the Japanese
realized what they were missing and passed a law which
emancipated cats and, you might say, nationalized them. The
Kyoto authorities ordered placards posted everywhere, carrying the decree that the cords on all cats were to be untied and
the cats freed. The purchase and sale of cats was forbidden
and heavy fines were levied on violators of the law.*

Back in Europe cats had traveled far and in a diversity of
ways.

The first northern people to keep cats were the Scots, and
this is how they got them: Fergus I of Scotland was descended

* M. W. de Visser, *The Dog and Cat in Japanese Superstition.*

from Galthelus, a Greek, who was commander-in-chief of the
Egyptian army when Moses led the children of Israel out of the
land of Egypt. Galthelus survived the destruction of the Egyptian army in the Red Sea, and with his wife Scota, who was
Pharoah's daughter, fled to what is now Portugal. There they
founded and ruled the Kingdom of Brigantium. More than a
thousand years later their descendant, Fergus, sailed into the
north and became the first King of Scotland, giving Scota's
name to the people and eventually to the land, bringing the
distant offspring of Pharoah's daughter's cats to the high-
lands.

To primitive Scots, puss was not merely the guardian of the
granary; puss was a mighty warrior. Even now you must guess
from the context whether a Scot is talking about a cat or a
fighting man, for *cat* means both, as it did when Fergus was
king. The crests and mottoes of highlanders descended from
the old Clan Cattan bristle with common battling cats. County
Caithness is the County of the Cats. The Duke of Sutherland
is still the Diuc Cat, the Duke of Cats. And the bagpipes of
the ladies from hell still caterwaul like wrathful toms.*

Cats must have reached the Netherlands almost as early, for
the Romans found a tribe at the old mouth of the Rhine who
called themselves the Cat People. The Roman stronghold, Lugdunum Batavorum, was built on the shore near the ancient
town of Cat Vicense. Lugdunum Batavorum was destroyed by
the sea long ago and Cat Vicense stands on the shore now, its
name restored to the language of the Cat People and called
Katwyk, Cattown. If you stand on the shore at Katwyk when
the tide is as low as it can be, you may be able to see the ruins
of the Roman fort.

Christianity and cats spread through Europe together. The

* C. R. (Caithness) Mackay, *The History of the Province of Cat.*

monasteries originated in Egypt and monks took their cats to the farthest ends of the known world.

One early disseminator of cats was a Scottish monk named Su Cat. *Su* in Gaelic means happy or good. *Cat* means either a warrior or a cat. Therefore Su Cat may be translated as the Happy Warrior or the Good Cat. Since Su Cat was a peaceful soul and a man of God, I think people knew him as the Good Cat. Su Cat journeyed from Scotland to the Western Isle, converted the people and exterminated the snakes that plagued them. His baptismal name was Patrick. Many of the earliest Irish churches are ornamented with carved stone cats, and I, for one, believe that Patrick's cats caught snakes for God. Before Patrick came, the Irish, having no cats, depended on rhyming the snakes away.

While the good monks were luring early Britons, Franks, Celts, and Gauls down out of trees, converting them and persuading them to wash off the blue paint, plant a crop, and keep a cat, barbarians were coming in from Asia, bringing rats and pestilence—there were no rats in Europe until they came. The barbarians were savages on horseback, who had no homes, raised no crops, and kept no cats. They burned, pillaged, looted, and plundered almost as far west as the Rhine, north to the Straits of Kattegat (the Cat's Gullet), and south to Rome. Rome fell and all roads led to ruin.

Some historians call the next six or seven hundred years the Dark Ages. This is more glib than accurate. Civilized Europeans fought the Vandal and the Hun, as the civilized world still fights them. Twenty-five million people died of the Black Death which scourged Europe for fifty years. The Black Death was bubonic plague brought in by the barbarians' rats. Otherwise the Dark Ages were far from dark.

In the towns that dotted the western coast from Spain to

Scandinavia, from Land's End to the tip of Caithness, and in the walled cities that marked the great overland trade route from the Mediterranean to the English Channel, people kept cats. Having cats to protect their property gave people security and time to think.

They began making their own laws, and abiding by them, instead of obeying Roman hand-me-downs. Welshmen and Saxons protected cats by law. Hoel dda of Wales promulgated a law fixing the price of cats: A kitling before it could see was worth a penny (and a penny was worth a whole lot more than it is today). Until it caught a mouse, a kitten was worth two-pence; when it commenced to mouse, fourpence. What's more, cats were sold with a money-back guarantee. If a Welshman bought a cat that was defective in any way, even a shiftless mouser, he could get a third of his money back. Anyone caught stealing or killing the cats that guarded the Prince's granary was obliged to forfeit a milk ewe, her fleece and lamb, or else was fined that amount of grain which would cover the dead cat when it was hung up by the tail with its nose touching the floor.

According to legend, Ap Madoc of Wales discovered America about the time the cat laws were promulgated. From the time of Noah mariners had steered by the stars with birds for com-passes, not daring to venture more than a bird's flight from land lest mice or rats destroy their goods and their food supply be-fore they touched shore again. Only after cats came to western Europe did little ships sail into the sundown. In the year 1000, Lief Ericson and his Vikings put out for Vinland, and not much later Breton fishermen began making yearly trips to the Grand Banks. Flavio Gioja perfected the compass, and men with compasses and cats circumnavigated the globe, explored and settled this continent.

While cats and men were happy around the fringes of

Christendom, it was right in the middle of Europe that cats outgrew their breeches and fell from grace.

Cats had long been cherished in Treves, Cologne, Coblenz, and other cities along the overland trade route, because they protected the storehouses which made living in cities possible. Outside the cities traipsing cattlemen, descendants of the barbarians, lived in wagons and drove their herds from grazing ground to grazing ground. They knew nothing about cats. When their women learned that by keeping cats people could settle down and get rich they went cat-crazy. They piled into the cities and towns, and before you could say scat the cat was a god again. The orgiastic rites of the cat-worshiping women of Egypt came alive again in Germany a thousand years after Cleopatra died.

The house-fraus of the Rhineland took to meeting in sacred groves when the moon was high and behaving like cats on a back fence. They revived the ancient Freya cult, which Christianity had extirpated from the cities long before, and gave Freya, the goddess of love and fertility, a brand new chariot drawn by cats. In this chariot Freya did some extensive gallivanting, down into Italy and over into France. When twilight finally settled on the gods of old, she attended the funeral of Baldur, the god of lusty youth, in her cat wagon. Thus the cat was lifted, tooth, claw, and whisker, into Valhalla.

The doings of the cat worshipers became a scandal throughout Christendom. Priests, monks, bishops, and popes preached against cat worship, only to spread it, as talk always does. Then, in 1484, Pope Innocent VIII empowered the Inquisition to search out cat-and-Freya worshipers and burn them as witches.

That was when the cat fell from grace.

Tens of thousands of people were executed as witches, many

of them simply because they lived with cats. In the German states alone, more than a hundred thousand people were legally executed—probably more than ten per cent of all the women in Germany died, and with them uncountable millions of cats.

Cats were legally condemned to be dipped in oil and set afire, thrown from towers on special feast days, beaten to death with whips and lashes and knotted ropes. Cats were crucified and scalded and skinned alive for the crime of being cats. *Omnia ad majorem Dei gloriam.* Our Lord must have wept to see it.

Cat hating and witch hunting spread beyond the Church and down the years. During Oliver Cromwell's Commonwealth sixty-odd witches were burned in England. Eighty years later witches were being burned in Scotland. New England had its witch hunts, and as late as 1800 accusations of witchcraft were made in South Carolina.

Cat hating became a cult and cat killing a sport. The good people of Denmark used to nail a cat in a barrel, hang the barrel between two trees, and ride full tilt at it, lance in hand. The noble Dane who shivered the barrel and killed the cat won the tournament and became the Cat King. In England cats were hung in leather sacks for bowmen to shoot at. With true Gallic finesse, the French invented the cat-organ, which when "played" caused one trapped cat after another to scream in agony. The cats were chosen for tonal variation and the effect was said to be most amusing. There were indeed more ways to kill a cat than by choking it on butter.

During the Inquisition and for a long time afterward people who didn't hate cats were in a fix. If they kept cats they'd be denounced as witches. If they tried to get along without cats the rats would eat them out of house and home. Those who escaped starvation and the stake had to explain their luck to hungry, envious neighbors. So ingenious people concocted the goblins, and in the midst of persecution the cat that had been twice a god became a godling, a kabouterje, a colfy, a goblin.

Nothing quite like the goblins ever had existed before. The world always was full of fairies, elves, banshees, and other spirits. The goblins were real. Their nearest relative was Kobalos, a Greek gnome who gave them their name. Kobalos was a glum little cuss who lived in mines and chipped away at ores and didn't do anything for anybody. His changeling offspring swept the kitchen, churned the butter and caught mice for considerate people who set out bowls of milk for them at night. Neglectful people found their yarn snarled into hag-knots, their milk spilled, or heard strange moanings all night long.

The goblins spread like toadstools after a rain, and everywhere they were the godlings of the kitchen and the barn, as cats had been before they rose too high and fell from grace. The goblins were about the size of cats. They all drank milk. They all caught mice. They all played impish tricks. They weren't cats, of course—dear me, no! The goblins wore stocking caps, green or brown jerkins and shoes that turned up in front, just like the common people who created them at the time of the Inquisition.

In Holland the cat-gnome was called Kabouterje; in France, Gobelin; in Germany, Kobold; in Russia, Colfy; in Wales, Coblyn; in England, Goblin; all namesakes of Kobalos. (The cobbler who mends your shoes also gets his trade name from Kobalos, because he's forever tapping.) In Scotland the goblins were known as Brownies because they wore dull English clothes instead of the plaid. To this day some highland women set bowls of milk on the Brownie stone at night.

The Norwegians, Swedes, and Lapps were far removed from the Inquisition and needed less disguise, so they called their goblin Smierragatto, the Buttercat. Smierragatto brought milk, bread, and money to its people, asking in return only a bowl of milk. In Finland, Smierragatto was known as Haltia. Haltia lived in the rafters, brought good luck and took care of household chores. When a Finn built a new house he always took along the rooftree and a shovelful of ashes from the old fire to please Haltia (everybody knows that an uneducated cat would rather use the fireplace for a toilet than go out). Haltia drank milk and when visible looked just like a cat. The Esthonian Puck was identical.

Everywhere the goblins went, Puss in Boots was sure to follow. From Italy to Scandinavia, Puss helped poor millers to fame, fortune, and fair lady. Inquisition or no Inquisition, the miller had to have cats because he was paid in kind: a tenth of all the grain he ground was his to sell, and if rats and mice got into it he wouldn't be a miller long. An honest miller had a hard time at best, what with paying rents to the landlord and tithes to the Church, and in the Low Countries where water power did not exist he even had to buy the Right of the Wind to turn his mill. He simply couldn't have rats. Millers did much to help cats survive the days of witchcraft.

Practically all of our anticat superstitions originated during the Inquisition, and you, my dears, who believe that cats bring bad luck, suck babies' breath, have nine lives, or any other such nonsense, hark back to the Inquisition and its practices.

The Inquisition was at its height when Columbus sailed, and cats were seldom mentioned in the early chronicles of America. Father Sagard, one of the first French missionaries, gave a cat to a Huron Indian and thought it important enough to write home about.* The cat would have been even more important to the Indian if he had appreciated it. The Indians were nomads

* *The Jesuit Relations.*

who sort of wished they weren't. They built houses and planted crops, and then, no matter what they did, the rodents came and ate their food stores and they were forced to go back to hunting and traipsing. If the Indians had had cats the history of America might have been different.

The *Encyclopedia Americana* is the only publication I ever saw that gave credit to cats for their help in colonizing this continent. Here is what it says: "The influence of the domestic cat upon American civilization has received less consideration than it deserves, for a great deal of the advance of agriculture as well as of the spreading out over the vast woodland and prairies has been made possible by this much-abused and misunderstood animal. How much food cats have saved, how much property they have guarded from destruction, what plagues of vermin they have kept in check from the time America was first settled, it is impossible to compute."

After the settler and his gun had routed the Indians, and the settler and his ax had cleared the wilderness, the settler's cats made homes possible where wilderness had been. On this continent there were forty major groups of rodents with seven hundred and fifty sub-varieties, all waiting for a farmer to come and raise a crop. There were wood rats, pack rats, field mice, rabbits, woodchucks, chipmunks and the rest of the natives— plus black rats, brown rats, roof rats, and mice from Europe.

Squirrels were the peskiest of all. In 1749 Pennsylvania Colony alone paid bounties on 640,000 gray squirrels, or about twice as many as there were people in Pennsylvania. The pioneers in Kentucky used to say that as soon as they planted a crop, squirrels swarmed down from the Indian country to the banks of the Ohio River, tore strips of bark from the trees, dragged them to the water's edge, jumped on, h'isted their tails for sails and were wafted over to Kaintuck. Only men with guns could deal with that invasion. But once the crop was in the barn a rifle was no mortal use, for the squirrels hid in the corn and ate both night and day, so cats were absolutely necessary. That's why every Scottish peddler in those days had a cat and kittens atop the load of pots and pans, needles and pins, books and tinker's tools he toted through the wilderness.

Cats were worth cash money or any reasonable swap when America was young. The first cat brought to Cuyaba, Paraguay, was sold for a pound of gold—about $560.00. Herrera the Conquistador paid more than $600.00 for the first cat brought to Peru. During the gold rush days in California the S.S. *Ohio* put in at San Francisco with a hundred-odd cats that had been bought for a dime apiece, and there they fetched ten and twenty dollars each.

About fifty years ago Memphis, Tennessee, had a plague of rats. Rats attacked people on the streets and bit babies in their cribs. The town had become almost uninhabitable when a man across the river in Arkansas advertised rat traps guaranteed to catch a rat a day, price one dollar. The frantic people of Memphis swamped him with orders—and got cats. They were furious and there was talk of jailing the rat-trap man for fraud. Before the talk developed into action the cats had cleaned up and Memphis was fit to live in once more. They still like cats in Memphis.

We never did have enough cats in this country. We haven't got enough now, though the New York A.S.P.C.A. kills almost five hundred unwanted cats a day. Mind you, they're not unnecessary cats, they're unwanted cats that have been abandoned in vacated stores, turned out to starve, left behind by allegedly civilized people who think it's bad luck to take the cat along when the family moves. If we realized the cost in money, food, and health of maintaining rats in luxury, we'd find homes for those cats.

According to the American Medical Association there are at least two rats for every human being in the United States, and this estimate does not include mice, which are considered uncountable. Rats and mice spread fleas, lice, mange, worms, and a number of deadly diseases, including bubonic plague which even now breaks out with disturbing frequency in our coastal cities, where rats are most numerous.

Also, our three hundred million rats destroy about six hundred million dollars worth of food every year—as the ancient Egyptians pointed out, what rats do not eat, they foul. This means that each of us, even nice people who live with cats, has to chip in four dollars every year to feed the rats. Now it seems to me we might put that money to better use. We could buy cat meat with it.

III

Nine Ways to Get a Cat

CATNIP IS ONE WAY

You could get a cat by planting catnip in the yard. The trouble is that you'd get other people's cats, maybe a dozen or fifty of them, and scarcely anyone wants a dozen or fifty cats.

OR YOU MIGHT FIND A CAT

Some people find cats all the time. Other people go through life without ever finding a cat. A good cat finder is an opportunist with a sharp eye for misery, the social conscience of a Robin Hood, and the stubbornness of a Republican in Texas.

Cat finding is an adventurous game with few rules: You don't "find" just any handsome cat you see sunning itself on a doorstep; that's somebody's cat and well you know it. You don't "find" a cat that's walking down the street minding its

Some people find cats all the time

own business; if it isn't somebody's cat it doesn't want to be. You don't "find" the butcher's cat or the grocer's cat or any other store cat. Store kittens may be "found" only on Sunday and only if the store is closed and the kitten is locked out. Only kittens or cats in distress should be "found"—I'll not be a party to cat stealing. Cats may be found legitimately in all sorts of places. Not long ago a homeless little cat was found in the subway, having kittens beside the roaring trains, a few inches away from the third rail. A woman I know found a kitten on Fifth Avenue, and I found a kitten on the steps of the Museum of Natural History. I "found" another kitten as it was being kicked out of a drug store by the proprietor, who had just thrown scalding soup on it. I found Charlie in a busy lumber yard where he had been abandoned. Lots of men find cats at night. Each tells the same story: He's coming home with a sandwich and a bottle of beer, sees a scrawny cat pawing at a garbage can, says, "Poor little devil," and keeps going. His feet begin to drag. He remembers how big that sandwich seemed when Henry was making it. He looks around; the cat is still pawing. He pinches the sandwich; it is a whopper. He starts back, feeling pretty silly. The cat has found a dry crust and is crunching loudly, perhaps a mite ostentatiously. He gives the cat half of his sandwich. The cat gulps it down, bread, lettuce, and all. He gives the cat the rest of the sandwich and buys himself another one. The cat follows him home. By all the rules of the game he has found a cat.

A found cat usually is a female with fleas, worms, rickets, and incipient kittens. By the time it has been fed, wormed, de-fleaed and delivered, it's something pretty special in the eyes of the person who found it. Some of the nicest cats I ever knew were found cats.

OR A CAT MIGHT FIND YOU

I can't tell you how to be found by a cat because that's a secret cats keep to themselves. I do know that the cats which choose their own people are the smartest cats of all. When a cat finds you, you may be sure it is a feline of discrimination, judgment, and taste.

Out of all the millions of people who pass on the streets of New York, Francie chose the two most likely to appreciate him and followed them home. The fact that they disliked cats and ignored him would have discouraged a weaker character than Francie. It was a challenge to him. He warped in and out between their feet, and shouted after them when the door closed in his face. The next evening he ambushed them, swooped out with clamorous greeting and raced ahead to wait at their front door. Again they shut him out. The third evening they found Francie waiting outside the door to their apartment. The fourth evening they looked for Francie; he wasn't on the street, or on the stoop, or in the hall. He was asleep on their living room sofa. How he got in remains a mystery to this day. The point is that he stayed and convinced his folks that cats were swell.

The Missus, as you know, found me, and after seven years I still feel absurdly proud that she trusted me with her kittens.

If a cat finds you, be nice to it.

THERE ARE GIFT CATS

You never can tell who will give you a cat. People who find cats work them off on their friends; after all, that's one thing friends are good for. People with too many kittens work them off on any nice person they meet. Some people I know came

home one night to find a policeman on their doorstep. After
the first anxious flutter, they saw he was holding a grubby
kitten. He'd been seeing it all evening, he explained. He'd fed it
some milk, but this was a cold night. Small cat; seemed a shame
for it not to have a home. . . . They've still got it. People with
spare kittens to give are as persuasive as a real estate agent
with a cut-over swamp on his hands.

YOU COULD BEG A KITTEN

Almost anyone can beg a kitten from the butcher, the grocer,
the delicatessen man, or the janitor.

The butcher's kitten is your best bet. In the hardest of hard
times the butcher's cat eats well and the butcher's cat's kittens get a good start in life. The butcher's cat is smart because
she works for a living and is well fed. Smart cats usually
raise smart kittens.

Next to the butcher's kitten, the grocery kitten and the delicatessen kitten run neck and neck; or, rather, egg and egg, for
both owe brains and beauty to the fact that eggs are both fragile
and nourishing. Intelligence and food are more closely related
than some of us realize.

The janitor's kitten is a gamble; better take it just before its
mamma stops feeding it and the janitor begins.

YOU COULD ADOPT AN ORPHAN

In all large cities and many small ones there are homes for
indigent cats, and people who wish to do good may go there
and adopt cats. I'd read the chapter on buying a cat * pretty
carefully and apply the rules as strictly as if the cat orphanage

* See page 35.

were a pet shop, if I intended to get a cat that way. I've known some mighty nice cats that came from the orphans' home. Of course you'll contribute something toward the support of future indigent cats.

CHILDREN WILL BRING CATS IN

They're not exactly found cats, just dragged in. For some strange reason children's cats are all alike, all limp, all dirty, all hungry, and all gentle.

Junior's cat may not grow up to be a cat you'd point to with pride; but then it isn't your cat.

Children take their cats seriously. The fact that Junior already has "a hundred-dollar dog" in no way affects his devotion to the bedraggled cat that took up with him in some back alley. That cat is his own personal discovery and no animal you can buy will ever be quite so close to his heart.

If you get rid of the first cat Junior brings in, he'll find another, and another. (Maybe he'll find somebody's cat, and then you'll be in a fix.) If you keep on getting rid of them he'll become frustrated and resentful and may grow up to hate you.

Don't pretend that it's all right for Junior to keep his cat, and then the moment his back is turned phone the humane society to come and get the cat. You won't fool your child, you'll merely prove that you're unreasonable, untrustworthy, and deceitful.

You cannot solve the problem by getting rid of the alley cat and buying Junior a fancy cat with a pedigree; he didn't want another cat, he wanted his cat.

If you're smart you'll help Junior to clean up his cat, and teach him to feed and brush it. In two or three months you'll probably find that his cat is handsome and pleasant and useful.

For some reason children's cats are all alike

SHOULD YOU GIVE A CHILD A CAT?

This, I think, depends entirely on the child. Theoretically, all children should have cats. Actually, some children are too rough to have any small animal, and mauling a kitten to death won't change the child's nature. I wouldn't go and buy a kitten for a very small child; and yet I was given a kitten when I was about a year old, and Snowball and I were devoted friends. I have since been told that Snowball was unattractive, grubby, and unfriendly to grownups—a typical child's cat.

I think the time to give a child a cat is when the child asks for a cat, or brings in a cat of its own choosing and shows a wish to keep it. I know a little boy who is going to get a kitten almost any minute. Six months ago I'd have skinned his parents if they had suggested a kitten for Rickey. He was a savage then, and the more he loved the rougher he was. Rickey is three now and his passions are mellowing into tenderness.

Cats and children make wonderful companions because cats have sense enough to go climb a tree when the play becomes too boisterous. They keep themselves clean, don't smell even when they're wet, and are very, very gentle with their children.

THE JOES

I don't know how to classify the Joes, except to say that their coming must be counted as one way to get a cat.

That summer I was busy and worried and had no time to play with cats. Ma and Pickle found ways to amuse themselves. Charlie got lonesome. He spent most of his time outdoors. So long as he came home to supper I didn't wonder where he'd been and never dreamed that he was lonely. Then one afternoon Charlie came up the stairs from the garden, very slowly, looking back at every step, making odd small chirruping chuckles. Behind him, in his shadow, came a skinny black kitten. Charlie led the kitten to the ice box, sat down and peeped at me, then he chirruped at the kitten, then he looked at the refrigerator. I fed the kitten. I called it Joe. The next afternoon Charlie came in with his Joe, and a second, identical Joe followed Charlie's Joe. The third day there were three Joes.

I did some unofficial investigating and learned that the Joes had had a mamma and a home, but their people moved away and took the mamma cat and left the Joes on the town. The Joes were scarcely old enough to be weaned, let alone old enough to shift for themselves, so . . . What would you do? It took me six long months to find homes for the Joes.

YOU COULD BUY A CAT

People buy cats for a number of reasons, the commonest of which is that fancy cats are more beautiful or outwardly more interesting than ordinary cats. Certainly no back-fence tabby can hope to match the elegance of a well-bred longhair, the stylized grace of a Siamese, or the comical rumpiness of a Manx cat. Other people buy cats because less conventional methods of acquiring them seem a bit shady—which no doubt they are—or because they're accustomed to buying pets, or because some winsome bit of fluff in a pet shop window won their heart. Whatever the reason, it is advisable to know something about the breeds of cat and the characteristics of a healthy kitten.

IV

How to Buy a Cat

WHAT KIND OF CAT?

First you decide what kind of cat you'd like to live with. This subject is of interest only to you, to the other members of your household, to the person who gets your money, and to the cat that comes to live with you. Tell your friends you're going to buy a cat and they'll swamp you with advice. They'll tell you that Persians are stupid, that Siamese "die often," that Manx cats are part rabbit, that Maine cats are part raccoon and goodness knows what else. If you believe them you'll probably go nuts and wind up with no cat.

In so far as the breeds of cat are concerned this is strictly one world. People have been meddling with cats for four thousand

35

years and they haven't been able to breed extra large cats or extra small cats or even lop-eared cats. There are rumors of lop-eared cats in China but no one, not a single Chinese, not even a cat-fur dealer has produced a single lop-eared cat for Occidental eyes to see. Cats in Egypt four thousand years ago looked about like cats in Evansville today. The peculiarities which distinguish the different breeds of cat are improvements that cats thought up for themselves. People can't take credit for creating Persians or Siamese or Manx cats or any other kind. At most we can claim to have perpetuated family resemblances, such as the taillessness of Manx cats, or coaxed Persians to grow longer hair, and even long hair is largely a matter of food and climate. People simply can't tell cats what kittens ought to look like.

The peculiarities which distinguish the breeds of cat, such as blue eyes, chocolate masks, long hair and taillessness, are merely variations which isolation, sometimes combined with climatic conditions, has fixed as types. In every instance the distinguishing peculiarity is recessive and common, ordinary cat is dominant.

Cross a Manx cat with a common cat and you get common kittens, with tails of sorts. Once in a while there's a tailless throwback to keep the rabbit-cat stories alive.

Cross a Persian with a common cat and you get mostly common kittens. One or two may turn out fluffy, but not fluffy enough to fool a cat-show judge.

Cross a Siamese with a common cat and you get common kittens, probably black, certainly not Siamese.

And, this one is tricky, cross a Siamese with a Persian and you get, not Siamese or semi-Siamese, not Persians or pseudo-Persians, not even a blending of Siamese and Persian; you get common, ordinary kittens.

When you consider that a hundred generations of "pure

breeding" can be wiped out in an evening's stroll when the moon is high, and that every female cat lives to take that stroll, the wonder is that there are any pedigreed cats for anyone to buy.

That's why you pay from ten dollars or so up to several hundred for a pedigreed cat. Any time a healthy, pure-bred kitten is sold for less than twenty-five dollars the breeder loses money on the deal. The breeder has to feed the mamma cat the year round. The kittens tucked away some milk and eggs and meat while they were being weaned. A stud fee was paid to some other breeder; or, if the breeder of your kitten kept a stud cat, the cost of feeding him just about balanced the money saved by not paying a stud fee. A veterinarian was called in at least once, and there were dozens of little inconsequential expenses that added up. There's twenty-five dollars accounted for, with little or no allowance for emergencies or work. If cat breeders charged for their work, goodness knows what kittens would cost.

THE BREEDS OF CAT

The following is a brief description of the breeds of cat that may be bought in the United States. It is intended as an elementary guide for people who wish to buy fancy cats and haven't quite made up their minds what kind. It is not intended for professional cat fanciers. And it is not intended for people who have had extended relations with cats. If I bred cats I'd breed for brains and wouldn't give a hoot what they looked like.

LONG-HAIRED CATS, KNOWN AS PERSIANS OR ANGORAS

Long-haired cats are beautiful in an expensive way that convinces the purchaser he's getting his money's worth. Because they are so lushly elegant, long-haired cats appear to be useless. They're not. No cat is useless unless people force it to be.

One of the smartest cats I ever knew was a big red Persian named Rube who helped to run a gas station. While the boss fixed cars Rube dozed in the screened shed behind the pumps, amid soft drinks, chocolate bars, and hang-over cures. When a car stopped Rube would yawn, stretch, and hook his claws into the rope that dangled above his cushion. The bell would clang in the workshop and the boss would come out front. He said Rube saved him the hire of a man.

I know a city Persian who is an expert mouser, to the envy and admiration of the bulldog she lives with. The bulldog is no kind of mouser; if he does happen to catch one it runs out between his teeth and the cat gets it.

All in all, long-haired cats are about what you give them a chance to be; it's pretty hard for a kitten to grow up smarter than its people.

The first long-haired cats came from Angora and were called Angora cats. Then we got mad at the Turks, who owned Angora, and began calling long-haired cats Persians. Nowadays the tendency is to call them all long-haired cats and let it go at that.

The first cats from Angora were stringy-haired and sharp-nosed. Selective breeding and good food fixed up their coats and a dash of alley cat broadened their skulls, and possibly their minds. The original strain is almost extinct. Nowadays anyone offering Angora cats for sale hasn't kept up with the world, or thinks the customer hasn't. The cats offered for sale as Angoras, not as Persians, are pure-bred Persians that didn't turn out right, or half-bred kittens that turned out better than expected. They are perfectly good cats, provided they are healthy; but the misrepresentation is dishonest and is practiced solely to wangle a few extra dollars. Don't pay Persian prices for kittens with Angora labels.

A healthy Persian kitten looks like a powder puff on a rampage. It should have a flat little pansy face, with wide-apart eyes, and ears well spaced. It should be so fuzzy that it seems almost square. It should love the whole world and everybody in it.

A black long-haired kitten is not as black as a black long-haired cat. It may even be a trifle rusty and still grow up inky black; on the other hand, it may grow up rusty. Kittens of other colors do not change at all. The kitten's coat is softer than the cat's coat, and markings that seem a little blurred in the kitten may sharpen; but the color won't change, spots won't go away, nor will stripes appear. Don't let anybody tell you different.

A full-grown Persian should be all fluff and frills, with a large round head, big round eyes, short snub nose and a Union League Club expression. Underneath the fluff and ruff there should be a sturdy, big-boned cat, with a short back, short legs, short neck and short tail. That square frame, which would be downright ugly in a short-haired cat, is what gives a long-haired cat its style. A Persian's fur should be long all over, with an extra-enormous ruff around the neck and down in a deep V between the forelegs. The tail should be bushiest at the tip.

To get anywhere in a show, a Persian should have eyes that contrast with the color of the coat. White Persians should have amber or blue eyes (and blue-eyed white Persians are practically all stone deaf). Blue Persians should have amber eyes, and so on.

Long-haired cats may be white (without streak or spot or trace of creaminess), black (the black of jet with the sheen of a blackbird's feathers), blue (blue-fox color without shade or stripe), chinchilla (white as new snow, each hair dark-tipped the least little bit so the whole cat glints like a bucketful of diamonds), cream (from the pallor of whipped cream on a restaurant pie to the richness of eggnog, but no nutmeg, no stripes), red (preferably copper color, but sometimes just plain yellow-cat yellow), tortoise-shell (black, orange, and yellow in about equal quantities, patched and pied with abandon), tortoise-shell and white (underneath the cat is white and it wears a Joseph's coat of tortoise-shell, a pied cap and a neat white collar. For no reason known to man 99.999999999 per cent of all tortoise-shell and tortoise-shell-and-white cats are females), smoke (the undercoat is silver-bright, the over-hairs sooty black, the ruff and frill smoky, the whole stripeless and spotless as smoke from a factory chimney). Last, there are tabbies. A tabby cat is not, as some people believe, necessarily a female. Tabby is not a corruption of Tabitha, and Tabitha is not the traditional name for a she-cat, as Tom is for a male. Tabby means "the silken one," and comes from the French "tabis," which in turn derives from the Italian "tabi," and it goes back to the Arabian "attabi," or the Persian "retabi," which is a very rich kind of water-figured silk that was woven long ago in Bagdad and was the only man-made thing that could compare with the silken-softness of a cat's fur. By rights, striped cats of either sex are tabby cats because of their moire coats. There are silver tabbies, red tabbies, orange tabbies, and brown tabbies, and each must be striped just so. Of course, cats may be other colors and combinations of colors, but if so they won't win any ribbons.

It seems to me that the people who breed cats make their job just as difficult for themselves as possible. If you're buying a cat because cats are fun to live with, an extra stripe or a fifth ring on the tail won't hurt anybody, and it will reduce the price of the cat.

In buying a long-haired kitten or cat avoid those which have skimpy coats, close-set eyes, ears too high on the head, or tails that taper to a point—that is, if you're set on winning one of those cat-show prizes. On the other hand, if you fall in love with such a cat, and won't grieve for the blue ribbons it can't win, go right ahead and buy it.

You'll be happier with a feisty, squint-eyed, stringy-haired caricature of a Persian cat with which you are spiritually in accord than you'd be with the grandest grand champion that ever purred if it wasn't also a friend of yours.

SIAMESE CATS

The Siamese is a cat lover's dream, lean and elegant, with sapphire eyes in a dark-masked face, a glamour puss if ever there was one, and smart as the dickens. Siamese cats have a special charm, exotic and aloof and totally without snobbery, which sets them apart from other cats. Also they are kind and loving and devoted to their people.

Siamese cats are extra smart and I never have known a crazy one. In time, if enough people breed them for beauty alone, I suppose a crazy strain * will develop somewhere and ignorant or unscrupulous breeders will perpetuate it. I certainly hope not.

Siamese cats are not held sacred in Siam, as some ardent fanciers would have us believe. They are the cats of the country, loved and respected as cats everywhere should be, no more, no less. Pale ones are highly valued because the Siamese people, who are Buddhists, esteem all light-colored animals. Indeed, the common people bow to every white animal they see, on the off chance that it might be Buddha himself, dropping in for a visit. There are some ordinary cats in the country in addition to the breed called specifically Siamese.

All good Siamese cats are marked alike. They have dark face masks and ears, dark feet, legs, and tails. The body color is pale and uniform and contrasts with the markings. The hardiest and least expensive are cocoa-colored cats with bitter-chocolate markings; they are also the largest. The body color of others varies through fawn to palest cream, with seal-brown points.

* See discussion of crazy cats.

Occasionally there is a silvery-blue Siamese with dark gray-blue markings. Because they are rare, blue-point cats are much admired and very expensive, although they are not quite so hardy as cats with seal-brown or chocolate points.

All Siamese cats darken in color as they grow older.

The palest kitten does not always grow up to be the palest cat.

All Siamese cats should have deep, clear, sapphire-blue eyes, which are very beautiful indeed. Those with greenish or yellowish eyes are handicapped at cat shows. They see just as well and make just as good companions, of course. Siamese cats hear at least as well as any other cat. Only blue-eyed *white* cats are born deaf.

Many Siamese cats are cross-eyed; this looks cute and isn't a fault.

Lots of Siamese have funny tails; three-quarters of a tail, half a tail, or kinked or knotted tails. Cat-show judges don't look down on Siamese cats with peculiar tails, because all oriental cats are haphazard about their tails.

The ideal Siamese cat is slim, rather long bodied, and at the same time compact, so the general effect is streamlined and powerful. The body color should be as even as paint on a wall, and the markings should be very dark. The head is longish and perfectly wedge shaped. From whiskers to tail the whole cat is smooth, glossy and well groomed. The expression is thoughtful, alert, and inscrutable.

Off-color eyes, a short neck or any suggestion of dumpiness detract from the cat's style.

If you buy a female Siamese cat be prepared to raise kittens or go crazy. The banshees take wailing lessons from Siamese cats in heat.

Siamese kittens are tiny little mites when they are born. They develop slowly and should not be weaned until they are about four months old. Reputable breeders do not sell Siamese kittens less than four months old. Because they develop so slowly, Siamese remain kittens for a long time. At birth Siamese kittens are about the color of a peeled banana, with faint smudges where the dark points will develop. By the time the kittens are old enough to sell, their markings are developing and their eyes are as blue as they are going to be.

Siamese kittens are sturdy and easy to raise if they are fed properly, kept dry, and not forced to sleep in draughty places. They thrive best in ordinary country surroundings, without any special pampering.

MANX CATS AND OTHER TAILLESS CATS

In the Far East and on the Isle of Man, tailless cats are common. In this country tailless cats are so scarce that about once a year some newspaper editor with nothing better to do dusts off the rabbit-cat story and serves it forth on Monday morning, garnished with lettuce and imagination. You know the story: A normal cat had one kitten with great big ears, little or no tail, and hind legs like a jackrabbit. The kitten hopped like a rabbit, nibbled a lettuce leaf for the cameraman, and thereby proved that it was the offspring of a wayward cat and an adventurous rabbit. The story never mentions that the kitten has cat's claws, cat's teeth, cat's whiskers, cat's eyes, or that it catches mice, and rabbits, in its spare time. Thousands of otherwise fairly intelligent people read this drivel and believe forever after that there are rabbit-cats, when they should know nature isn't that careless. Did you ever hear of a goat-dog? Or a horse-cow? Or a pig-sheep? Of course you didn't! Leaving out all scientific considerations, how do you think the offspring of a rabbit and a cat could possibly combine its inheritance of basically dissimilar teeth and whiskers, eyes, feet and stomachs? It couldn't, that's all.

The tailless cats of Asia are practically unknown in the United States, so we who know better than to believe the rabbit-cat story call all tailless cats Manx cats. People who live on the Isle of Man speak of them as "The cats of the Spanish Rock," which seems to bear out the theory that the first ones came ashore there when the Spanish Armada was wrecked. Erudite people argue that tailless cats are, and always have been, unknown in Spain, so the cats of the Armada must have had tails. They seem to forget that the Armada was wrecked during Spain's great days, when Spanish ships had sailed the world around, and any Spanish sailor might have bought or swiped a couple of no-tail cats in Asia.

A typical Manx cat is smallish, bullet-headed, with a gentle, un-catlike expression, hind legs three sizes too large, and a dimple where its tail would be if it had one. In England, Manx cats are forthrightly called Rumpys, and fanciers strive to breed them rumpier and rumpier.

Quite frequently Manx cats disgrace themselves by having kittens with tails of sorts, usually peculiar. The good folk of the Isle of Man do their best to remedy this by docking the kittens' tails and selling the docked kittens to happy trippers as genuine Manx cats.

Manx cats waddle when they walk and hop like rabbits when they run.

Cat-show judges don't care what color Manx cats are, so long as they are rumpy and dimpled. Black, white, silver tabby, brown tabby, and blue tabby are common colors. Solid blue is rare; red, tortoise-shell, and spotted Manx cats are extremely rare. Theoretically, their eyes should contrast with the color of the coat. Actually, Manx cats are so scarce that you take what you can get.

MAINE CATS

Maine cats are perfectly charming, and not so well known as they deserve to be. Some people say they are a breed, and some say they're not. Their kittens grow up to look like them, so I say they're a breed.

No one seems to know how Maine cats originated, except that there must have been a Persian somewhere in the background. The most intriguing explanation I have heard comes from Mrs. Hendee Rice of Hartford, Connecticut, who heard it from a "Down-Easter." It seems, according to the lady from Down East, that they are descended from the cats brought by Captain Coon, who commanded the ship that brought over the furnishings for the house in Edgecombe, Maine, that was intended to be a refuge for Marie Antoinette. Consequently, they are called "coon (or Coon) cats, for the Captain." It is *not* because they are part raccoon. No cat can be part anything but cat.

Maine cats are big. They have large heads and intelligent, rather doggy, faces. The skull and nose are broad, and the whole head has a solid look which I find satisfying to the eye. The average Maine cat is about the size of a big common cat and not so lanky. You know you've hefted something when a Maine cat sits in your lap. Maine cats have long hair which lacks the ostrich plume elegance of Persians and hangs more like a collie dog's fur. The tail tapers to a point—the reverse of a Persian's tail.

Cat-show judges are not interested in Maine cats because they are not recognized as a breed, so there are no show points to look for or avoid; but I would not buy a Maine cat that had close-set eyes, a narrow skull or any suggestion of fox-face. Since they are not of the elite, Maine cats may have any kind of markings or combination of colors, because only the people they live with, and possibly other cats, care what color they are. Some Maine cats have beautiful parti-colored markings, like calico ponies. If ever I bought a cat, I think I'd buy a calico cat from Maine.

ABYSSINIAN CATS

I owe an apology to Abyssinian cats; when first this book was written I never had seen one. Now I have. The males are tall, slim and charming; the females petite and delightful. They are brown, ticked darker. They are very rare, very expensive, and I love them.

BLUE CATS

Call them Maltese, Russian, British blue, Australian or Carthusian cats, or make up a name if you like. Cat fanciers insist that short-haired blue cats are a separate breed, and not only a separate breed but all the separate breeds listed above. I am willing to agree that they are one separate breed. I am not willing to agree that they are half a dozen separate breeds because (a) I can't tell them apart, and (b) I don't think a long upper lip or a short neck constitutes a breed. If they'd call them Blue Cats, Russian type, British type, and so on, I would agree.

At present, if you get a blue cat that is long and lanky it's a Russian blue; if short and stocky it's a British blue. Somewhere in between you'll find the others.

The main thing about a blue cat is that it is blue all over, hair, whiskers, lips, soles of the feet, and even the skin should be the color of a blue fox fur; otherwise a cat fancier won't look at it. Markings are absolutely tabu, not a spot or a stripe allowed. Blue cats of all these "breeds" vary from pale silvery gray to dark slate color, with all shades between, including lavender gray. The color should be uniform with a frosty sheen and no rusty shadings on the back. Light blue is stylish at present. Goodness knows what shade will be fashionable next year.

Blue cats average rather small and perfectly charming. Charlie is a blue cat.

PLAIN CATS

A few people breed extra fancy short-haired cats and show them and sell them. This is strictly a labor of love and should not be undertaken by anyone with the slightest wish for profit. There is a small market for handsome, healthy short-haired cats, respectable with pedigree, and the market would grow if more people knew such cats could be bought. I know a woman who refused a common gift-kitten on the ground that its mamma might have been an immoral feline, and then went out and bought a kitten in a pet shop, though it was just as common and hadn't any pedigree either. This proves something about respectability and shows that people do buy plain cats.

Fanciers of short-haired cats have clubs and shows, with classes for cats of various ages and sexes and colors, just as Persian, Siamese, and Manx cat fanciers do. Every once in a while a cat that was picked up in some back alley and never heard of a Standard of Points goes to a cat show and wins over all the fancy cats, and people like me cheer wildly.

MALE OR FEMALE?

Male cats are handsome, females are pretty. Males are smart, females are wise. If you buy a female cat you can raise kittens, which is one of the most delightful avocations in the world. People who don't want to raise kittens should not buy female cats and thwart them; it's hard on the cats, and oh so much harder on the people.

Male kittens cost more than females. This is partly due to primitive superstitions of male superiority, and partly because most female cats come in heat often and vociferously. There are exceptions. One cat I lived with came in heat once a year and quietly went out and got herself some kittens. Other cats I've known came in heat three or four times a year, while some raised the roof every four weeks. If you let her have kittens this won't bother you much.

I really think the sensible thing to do is to buy the kitten you like best and let nature take its course.

KITTEN OR CAT?

It's all right to find a full-grown cat and marvelous to be found by one. I wouldn't buy an adult cat. I can't imagine how anyone would be willing to miss the fun of raising a kitten. Also, a cat that has grown up with other people may not wish to live with you. The fact that you paid money for the cat wouldn't mean you'd bought its love and loyalty. Cats don't understand commerce and probably would be disgusted with us if they did.

A cat that has lived with someone else for a year or more has fixed habits of its own, and standards of conduct for people. The cat's standards for people may be much lower than yours. It doesn't matter, that's what the cat expects and you'll be criticized all day long every day without knowing where you've failed. You'll end up feeling as embarrassed as the ladies in deodorant advertisements.

Let Nature take its course

Not uncommonly, cats pine away when they are separated from the people they have known and loved all their lives. Once long ago I gave away a cat I'd lived with for two years, and the imbecile woman I gave her to let her die of grief without even telephoning me. She said she didn't know cats died of grief. That cured me, and let it be a lesson to you.

If you're buying a breeding cat from a cattery and want the finest specimen money can buy, that's another matter. This book isn't written for people who buy specimens.

HOW MANY CATS?

Two cats, like two heads, are better than one. Unlike two heads, two cats are easy to get.

Living with two cats is about three times as much fun as living with a solitary cat. True, there are moments, when Ma, Pickle, and Charlie all pile in my lap at once, making a thirty-five- or forty-pound heap, that I feel three is a large number of cats. The rest of the time they're exactly right. When they romp like kittens it's hard to realize that Charlie and Pickle are almost elderly cats, while the Missus is probably old enough to vote.

I wouldn't keep brother and sister together without having one of them castrated or sterilized. The same thing applies to mother and son, unless the mamma cat is so downright marvelous that you want more kittens just like her—which you may or may not get, even with three or four generations of line breeding. The whole subject of genetics is so complicated and tricky that you'd better let the cat around the corner sire your kittens, provided he's smart and handsome.

If you have a cat and bring in a kitten, the old cat may be jealous for a while. Ignoring the kitten as far as possible (as if

*Criticized all day without knowing where
you've failed*

one could ignore a kitten!) and giving the old cat a lot of extra attention will cure the jealousy nine hundred and ninety-nine times out of a thousand.

You can't know how loving, intelligent, and genuinely unselfish cats are until you've lived with two or more at once. Just don't play favorites—it hurts their feelings and stirs up jealousy.

WHERE TO BUY A CAT

People buy cats at pet shops, cat shows, pet shows, from breeders who maintain professional catteries, and from anxious people who started out with a pure-bred female cat, bred her because she was driving them crazy and they might as well turn an honest penny anyhow, and now they've got kittens and an ad in the paper.

There is no foolproof method of buying a cat, and there are no foolproof cats. The generally accepted theory that a pet shop is the worst place to buy a kitten because pet shops are dirty is pure theory, nothing else. Most pet shops are clean, and the dirtiest pet shop is no dirtier than the dirtiest cattery; it couldn't be. In general, pet shops, pet shows, and cat shows are equally risky places to buy kittens; any place where a lot of cats are brought together is bound to have a germ or so about.

If you've set your heart on a really fancy cat, why not visit a cat show and collect the addresses of those breeders who have the handsomest cats. Then wait two weeks until all the cats that were going to catch anything at the show have caught it, and go look. If the cats didn't catch anything, that's the time to buy a kitten.

The anxious people with one cat, a litter of kittens and an ad in the paper are worth considering, too. They probably haven't a germ to their name.

Wherever you go to buy a kitten, let your nostrils be your guide. If you smell cat, get out. Don't stop to play with the kittens and pick up a disease to pass on to the next healthy kitten you meet. The rule of nose applies to any place where cats are offered for sale, even the nicest place. The smell may be only a healthy tomcat's indoor toilet, and then again it may not. Sick cats have an odor and only an expert can tell the difference.

If you can't smell cat, look around, and I mean *look*. If you see even one kitten with runny eyes and a gummed-up nose, get out! Don't stop to say, "Poor kitty, has it dot a cold in its 'itty heady?" If you do, you're inviting the proprietor to explain that he put flea powder on that one just a little while ago, not that it had fleas, it didn't of course, and that one always sneezes . . . and before you know it, you'll have a kitten with a runny nose, though the chances are you'll not have it long.

If your nose and your eyes say the place is all right, go ahead and choose your kitten.

HOW TO CHOOSE A KITTEN

Cats wean kittens when they are six or seven weeks old. After weaning they should be left with their mother a few days to learn the fine points of cat etiquette, which mamma cats teach much more efficiently than people. Kittens should not be sold until they are at least seven weeks old. Anyone who offers younger kittens for sale is not quite honest.

You can judge the age of a kitten by looking at its teeth. Don't pry its mouth open to look, for kitten bones are frail; play with it until it laughs. If you see that the baby teeth haven't broken through the gums, the kitten is less than four weeks old, and much too young for you to buy. If the teeth are beginning to show, the kitten is still too young. The kitten for you to buy has a full row of tiny, sharp, clean, white teeth in each jaw. The inside of a kitten's mouth should be a nice rosy coral, neither pallid nor scarlet.

A healthy kitten looks as unsubstantial as a dandelion. It weighs next to nothing and still feels firm and kicks like fury when you hold it. It is all over the place and into everything, or else tight asleep.

A kitten old enough to sell is quick and sure footed, and able to walk slowly as well as run. Kittens learn to run before they walk. A kitten that dashes across the floor, topples, picks itself up and toddles a few steps isn't old enough to leave its mamma.

A young kitten's coat is downy with a slight bloom, a sort of feathery glossiness, and it should look alive. The hard shine of the cat's coat does not appear until after the first molt, when the kitten is five or six months old. Never buy a kitten with a skimpy, patchy, dirty, dry, or dampish coat.

Feel the kitten all over, very gently, for skin blemishes, even if your best friend raised it. If you find any roughness part the hair and investigate. If it is obviously a scratch and healing, all right. If it is any other blemish, however slight, that kitten is not for you. Stories about milk rash, weaning rash or any other rash, flea bites, allergy, or "Oh, that's nothing, kittens always get that," are fairy tales pure and simple. The blemish or roughness could be (a) an injury, (b) a rash caused by worms, (c) a glandular disturbance, (d) ringworm, (e) mange, (f) something else that could cause trouble.

A healthy kitten's belly is nicely firm with some "give" in it, neither flabby nor hard. A hard, flabby, or swollen belly is an indication of worms, rickets, or some other ailment. It is not an indication that the kitten just ate breakfast. Even if it overate and its tummy was a little bit puffy, it wouldn't look swollen or feel hard.

Healthy kittens always have bright eyes, usually hazy blue. There is no rule governing the age at which a kitten's eyes change from baby blue to their permanent color. Pickle had beautiful violet-blue eyes until he was four months old, and Charlie's eyes became orange when he couldn't have been more than seven or eight weeks old. Never touch, let alone buy, a kitten with dull, running, or sticky eyes.

Look, do not feel or poke, inside the kitten's ears. They should be perfectly clean and entirely odorless.

If you're thinking of buying a white kitten, make sure it isn't deaf. As I've said, nearly all blue-eyed white cats are born stone deaf. Deaf-born cats learn to depend on their eyes to an astonishing degree, so don't fool yourself by making motions along with the sounds you use to test the kitten's hearing. If you do, you may not realize the cat is deaf until after it has met with an accident that a normal cat might have avoided.

The least kitten in a litter usually is the smartest, the weakest, and a female. Since I find the least kitten in almost any litter irresistible, I can't advise you not to buy a least kitten if you like it and it likes you.

A reliable breeder or dealer will tell the truth about the sex of the kittens he has for sale, but looking never hurt anybody. If you are one of those people who have difficulty in distinguishing the sex of kittens, take a good look at the kitten you like and ask to see a kitten of the opposite sex; don't be bashful about it, cats aren't. Knowing will save you the embarrassment of having to tell your friends that Oscar just had kittens. I never heard of anyone who was offered a female cat that turned out to be a male. If you should be offered a tortoise-shell or tortoise-shell-and-white kitten as a male, ask gently why its price is less than a thousand dollars. Tortoise-shell tomcats are slightly scarcer than hen's teeth.

It is possible to recognize the brightest kitten in a litter, and if there is a stupid one you can avoid it. The exceptional kitten identifies itself by its deviation from the average. Kittens don't become rugged individualists until they catch their first mice and cut their second teeth, and then they're cats. Kittens are as gregarious as children in the fourth grade. Every kitten in a litter wants to do what every other kitten is doing at that moment; they all get hungry at once, they all play at once, they all go to sleep at once. The smartest kitten is the ringleader. It may lead by a kitten's whisker—first to the milk, first on your shoulder, first into mischief. That kitten will grow up smart as a whip and a peck of trouble. It may be male or female, loving or indifferent, brilliant or plain smart; nobody will know for a while. If it's a genius you may not want it; some people are annoyed by brilliant cats.

On the other hand, you are not likely to want an idiot cat, or a crazy cat. If breeders weeded out moron kittens as conscientiously as they weed out kittens with an extra stripe on the left hind leg, there wouldn't be any abnormal fancy cats. I don't mean to imply that all pure-bred cats are morons, or even any sizable percentage of them. Neither am I suggesting that all idiot cats have pedigrees. In all probability as many imbecile kittens are born in alleys as on silken cushions. In the alleys adversity weeds out the stupid cats. In the planned economy of the cattery dim-witted kittens grow up, are sold, and, according to the brightness of the people who buy them, turn out to be passable or terrific disappointments.

Inbreeding usually is blamed for the disappointments. People do a lot of loose talking about the evils of inbreeding. Inbreeding is not an evil in itself—it is the only known way to fix types. All pure-bred cats are descended from long lines of closely related ancestors. The trouble is that when cats with blue eyes and three rings on the tail are fashionable, all the fanciers inbreed blue-eyed cats with three rings on the tail whether they've got any sense or not. If they are sane, sturdy cats, no harm is done, and possibly some good is accomplished because in this way sanity and sturdiness also are fixed as types. But if the best ring-tailed, blue-eyed stud happens to be on the dumb side, and he is mated to his litter sister, and their kittens are bred back to him or his sister or other close relatives, a family of feline Jukeses is bound to develop. The worst of it is that ring tails and blue eyes can vanish in a generation, while idiocy will stick until that strain of cats dies out.

By following a few simple rules you can avoid getting stuck with a fool cat or a crazy cat.

1. Do buy a kitten that runs with the crowd. If you think the ringleader might be troublesomely bright, take the kitten that is half a jump behind the leader, if you like it equally well.

2. Do buy a kitten that reacts normally to unusual sounds and such enchanting sights as a length of string being pulled across the floor.

3. Do buy a kitten that answers when it is called. By the time it can walk a kitten should know enough to respond to "kitty, kitty, kitty."

4. Do buy a kitten as sharp witted as the average in its litter.

5. Do buy a kitten that loves the whole wide world and you, especially you.

6. Do, above all, buy the kitten you like best, even if the seller says it hasn't a chance to win a ribbon. Buy it if it costs twice as much as you'd planned to spend, or if the price is so low you're sure its pedigree must be faked; pedigrees are darn poor companions.

Now the don'ts:

1. Don't buy a shy kitten, if it is ever so beautiful. Shyness

may be caused by illness or stupidity, and you don't want a sick or stupid cat.

2. Don't buy a kitten that bushes its tail and spits at imaginary enemies, unless you have a hankering to set up in business as a spiritualist with a spook-ridden cat. Anyway, the symptoms probably indicate nothing more occult than bad eyes, bad nerves, or a bellyache.

3. Don't buy a kitten that keeps itself to itself. It is against nature for a kitten to want to get away from it all.

4. Don't buy a kitten that doesn't like you. It must live with you at least until it gets a chance to leave home.

5. Don't buy a slow, sluggish kitten. If it isn't dim-witted it's ailing.

Kittens that cost money are healthier than alley kittens and not quite so sturdy. Generations of freedom from want and freedom from fear, of catnip mice and cream for breakfast, of monogrammed scratching posts and perfect sanitation, have produced beautiful cats that are able to cope with almost anything except disease. Of course a lot of aristocratic cats triumph over heredity and environment and win blue ribbons, catch mice and resist germs.

Tenderly reared cats are often handicapped by ignorance. A cat whose mice have all been stuffed with catnip can't teach kittens much about the art of mousing. Since Utopia for cats is still around the corner, a kitten educated to catch its own supper is better off than one conditioned to a life of subsidies and handouts. I'm not advocating hard times for cats, understand; I just don't want you to be surprised if your blue-blooded little darling thinks mice are charming companions.

If, in spite of all precautions, you buy a kitten and it dies, don't imagine that you should go back with a yelp that it was sick when they sold it to you and you want your money back.

Maybe the kitten was sick when you bought it. Probably it wasn't. If you've read this chapter carefully, you ought to be able to keep away from sick kittens. Anyway, nobody sold you a kitten—you bought it. Even your best friend would doubt that you were fool enough to go out and buy a sick cat. If anything goes wrong, tell the person you bought the kitten from; tell him nicely and I expect he'll help you. Start chanting, "The cat was sick when you sold it to me," and he'll probably throw you out.

V

How to Feed a Cat

TO COOK OR NOT TO COOK

Did you ever see a cat fry a mouse? Then why should you cook for a cat? Cooking, even for the likes of you and me, is a comparatively recent invention. Millions of people living in the world today never saw a stove; a sizable percentage of them never even saw a fireplace with a chimney. They cut their meat in chunks, impale the chunks on sticks which they hold over a fire until the meat begins to scorch; then they eat it, burnt on the outside, raw inside.

People cook meat because (a) it keeps longer, and (b) it tastes better. In these days of sanitation, refrigeration, and a butcher shop around the corner, preservation isn't much of a consideration, so most people cook meat to improve the taste. Where other methods improve the taste we still eat our meat raw. To wit: Westphalian ham, Italian prosciutto, chipped beef, and many other sorts of smoked, jerked, and dried meat, sausages, and fish.

Cats don't think cooked meat tastes better, and they'd rather preserve it inside them.

The notion that raw meat will give cats worms is an old wives' tale. Cats get various kinds of worms from rats, mice, fleas, lice, the grass blades they nibble in the back yard if worm larvae happen to be roosting on them, and even from their mammas, if mamma has worms. They can get trichinosis from raw pork and a certain sort of tapeworm from raw fish. They cannot get any kind of worms from government inspected beef, lamb, mutton, or veal fit for human consumption, whether it is done or raw.

A lot of people argue that feeding an animal raw meat will "make it vicious." If raw meat would make a cat vicious, cooked meat would too. Meat is simply protein, and the method of preparation cannot possibly affect the eater's disposition. The only thing that happens when a cat is fed raw meat is that it becomes a healthier, happier, and smarter cat than if it got meat with some of the good cooked out. Maybe you've noticed that the butcher's cat is smart—you didn't think butchers instinctively picked smart cats, did you!

STEAK OR SPINACH

There's also the cherished notion that the carnivorousness of cats is a vulgar habit which can be cured by means of a genteel diet of vegetables. Then, when the cat shows signs of malnutrition as a result of this genteel diet, a tonic seems to be the answer. The sort of person who feeds a cat vegetables isn't likely to select a sensible tonic, and the final result usually is a collection of empty bottles and a dead cat. People who disapprove of carnivorousness shouldn't try to live with cats.

The cat has long, sharp fangs to catch and kill its mice and other vermin, and sharp-edged molars to cut them to swallowing size. The cat has no flat-surfaced teeth with which to masticate crispy-crunchy cereals or peanuts or radishes. The strong front teeth which enable men, monkeys, and mice to gnaw raw apples and corn on the cob don't amount to shucks in a cat. If a cat should wish to eat an apple, it would have to bite off chunks with its back teeth—you try it some time!

Vegetarian animals have very long intestines to help them digest their corn and beans. Omnivorous animals have moderately long intestines. The carnivores have exceedingly short intestines, and cat guts are short even for carnivores. Cats' stomachs secrete digestive juices that make the most of any meat that comes their way, while trying to ignore dietary oddities. You can't reform a cat's stomach.

Cats, like all meat-eating creatures, chew grass and nibble an occasional strawberry (foxes do eat grapes, you know). Cats need small quantities of vegetables. House cats in particular need something green three or four times a week. A spoonful at a time is plenty because vegetables serve as a cat's spring tonic, a combination laxative-and-hairball-remover,* occasionally as an emetic. Any vitamins obtained thereby are strictly coincidental and are not to be confused with a piece of meat.

That dab of spinach left from dinner, the string bean Puss swiped while you were stringing them, the three or four peas she batted around the floor, a lettuce leaf and a sprig of parsley will last a cat a week. Or you might plant grass seed in a flower pot and let Puss graze at will. Cats like growing greens better than grocery store vegetables. They like them so much that it's

---

* See discussion of hairballs.

hard to keep ornamental plants and cats under the same roof unless you keep the plants in the cat, where they're not very ornamental. Cats just love ferns, petunias, nasturtiums, verbenas, marigolds, parsley, besides catnip, of course, and almost anything else a nature-loving person might wish to grow.

Cats are rather choosy about their food. A hungry cat gives you no peace until you feed it; when it has had enough to eat, it quits. I don't know anything more exasperating than trying to coax a cat to finish a perfectly good dab of meat, not enough to save and too much to throw away. The cat listens to your wheedling, watches politely to see if you're going to eat that bite yourself, decides you aren't, scratches all around the dish with the impersonal thoroughness of a streetsweeper, and walks away.

OVERFEEDING

Of course you can overfeed a cat if you set your mind to it. Choosy as they are, cats can be overfed, underfed and badly fed. They can be, and often are, shockingly misfed by people with the best intentions imaginable.

Overfed cats usually get too much of what is good for them, and get it too often. Most cats know when to quit. Very few cats know when to start. Feed a cat a big meal, give it a few hours to shake down, and the cat will be ready to eat again. A cat on its own catches a mouse, takes a nap and wakes up ready for another mouse, which it probably won't catch; certainly it doesn't find a mouse waiting to be caught every time it wakes up. If you provide the equivalent of half a dozen mice every time the cat feels peckish, you'll soon have a fat, lazy good-for-nothing on your hands.

The person who lives alone with a cat is most likely to overfeed it. First, you give the cat its breakfast, and the last bite of

Watches politely to see if you're going to eat it yourself

your scrambled egg. Then at lunch time you feel mean and selfish and greedy eating all alone while poor Puss watches every bite and wistfully begrudges it, so you give the cat a little liver pâté, or a speck of cream, or a chop bone that hasn't much meat on it anyway. And come dinner time Puss gets a big meal, with maybe a snack at bed time. I know how you feel, I've felt that way and I've stuffed a cat; but it isn't fair to the cat. The alternatives are to let the cat stare, which will spoil your own meal; lock it in the bathroom; or skip lunch—it probably wouldn't hurt you to skip lunch.

UNDERFEEDING

There is no excuse for underfeeding a cat. Cats don't ask much and they're pretty tolerant about your choice of food. People who aren't willing to spend a nickel a day on cat food don't want a cat and the sooner they get rid of it the better. Unfortunately, few if any such people will read this book.

MONOTONY

Monotony is almost as bad as starvation. I met a woman once who fed her cat canned shrimp and nothing else; you never saw a sorrier looking cat. People who feed cats the same thing day after day usually excuse themselves by saying they're not going to pamper a cat, or they haven't time to shop around, or, "It's good cat food, isn't it? Why shouldn't he have it every day?" Those same people complain that they are tired of roast lamb by the time it becomes hash. No one thing is all-satisfying enough to nourish any domestic animal indefinitely. The fact that a cat can drag along for months, or even years, on canned shrimp, or prepared cat food, or even liver, doesn't mean that it is satisfied or well nourished. It isn't.

FOOD FOR THE WORKING CAT

The worst-fed cats of all, oddly enough, are cats that work for a living. A stupid superstition has grown up in the minds of people who keep cats to catch vermin that a well-fed cat won't hunt. Those people know they can't do a good day's work if they're anemic, run down and weak, and how they expect a half-starved cat to be successful is beyond me. Common sense should tell them that starvation is weakening, and that weak, slow cats can't catch mice.

Only starving cats will eat rats, and starving cats don't catch many rats. Also, eating rats often makes cats sick and sometimes kills them. A cat that has once been made ill may starve to death rather than eat another rat. Rats are filthy, disease-carrying, dangerous creatures and we shouldn't permit cats to eat them.

Cats do eat mice. But a mouse is a very small animal and it takes a lot of mice to fill a cat. Any cat that has to depend entirely on the mice it catches is likely to go hungry most of the time.

The notion that cats can live on milk and what they catch is only slightly less crazy than the idea that cats can live on what they catch and no milk.

I don't think cats consider the vermin they catch to be food. I think they regard hunting as a profitable sport, or an enjoyable business—a paying hobby. Some cats are industrious hunters and some are not. Some are efficient mousers and are afraid of rats. Some are killing fools and some specialize.

Starvation will not turn an incompetent cat into a good

mouser, and starvation most certainly will ruin a good cat, or
any other cat.

WHAT TO FEED A CAT

Don't think you have to buy filet mignon; the cat would
just as lief have shin—liefer, probably. All the cheap cuts of
meat, plus the innards which people don't much like anyway, are good cat food. A cat that does its own hunting nearly
always eats the innards first, leaving the muscle meat for later,
if ever. Actually, a well fed cat should have organic meat, muscle meat, fish, eggs, and milk if milk agrees with it, more or
less alternated. Some cats like, and seem to need, a small amount
of cereal food, such as Tiny Bits, oatmeal, Cream of Wheat, or
one of the crispy-crunchy breakfast foods. One cat I know eats
Wheaties and milk for breakfast every day. Pickle would eat
a whole bag of Fritos if he could get them.

FATS AND OILS

Those of us who were living with cats ten years ago or more
accepted the theory that cats must not have any fat in their diet,
and scrupulously kept it from them. The theory was all wrong.
Cats require some fat to keep them in good condition, and fat
seems to help ward off kidney and bladder stones. I know of
two Siamese cats that eat a pound of Crisco every two weeks!
Cats that were brought up in the no-fat-for-cats days don't
take kindly to a change; the only way I can get fat into Pickle
is to pop a piece of cold butter in his mouth and hold it shut
while the butter melts and he has to swallow. The average
cat needs about a teaspoonful of fat a day: butter, beef suet, margarine or any other edible fat or oil.

INSIDES

Liver. Liver is the traditional cat food. I have known cats that lived to a ripe old age on liver alone; it wasn't a balanced diet, it wasn't a good diet, but it didn't kill them. I'm told that years ago butchers used to give liver away to people with cats because nobody would buy it. Now that we know how nourishing liver is, we eat it ourselves and say it's too expensive for cats. Calf liver is expensive food for anybody, and not a bit more nourishing than any other sort.

Many people consider pork liver unfit food for cats because raw pork can give a cat trichinosis. Trichinae live almost exclusively in the muscles of the pig, and glandular organs are not likely to be dangerous, but I would cook it, just the same. Cooked pork liver, like all cooked pork, is absolutely safe, and cooked pork liver is good cat food for a change.

When a cat is unaccustomed to a steady diet of liver its insides are startled when liver suddenly shows up. Liver as an occasional treat has two handicaps: raw liver acts as a laxative; cooked liver constipates. You can turn this to advantage by feeding the cat raw liver to correct constipation, and by using cooked liver to check diarrhea due to sloppy food, such as soups and stews, which aren't good for cats anyway.

Kidneys. The cats I live with like kidneys best of any food. They eat any kind with equal delight. Unlike liver, kidneys do not startle cats' insides.

Heart. Heart is very good cat food, cheap and nourishing. One kind of heart is as good as another.

Lungs and brains. Lungs and brains are more nourishing than they look. They look awful. Cut-up lungs look like bloody marshmallows. Brains are pallid and slippery.

Before the rationing of World War II made peculiar kinds

of meat a necessity for cats, I didn't consider such oddities food for anything. Then I discovered that cats had no such prejudice. Ma, Pickle and Charlie lived on lungs and brains, with fish and eggs as an occasional change, for a long time and stayed in beautiful condition. They were crazy about lungs. They were less crazy about brains.

Tripe. Tripe is said to be nourishing. I'm not so sure about that, and anyway cats don't like it. Tripe is listed solely for the record.

MUSCLE MEAT

While cats prefer innards, they thrive best on a diet composed partly of innards and partly of muscle meat, plus fish and eggs.

Beef. All cuts of beef are good for cats. If cheap cuts which contain little or no fat are fed, a teaspoonful of beef suet should be minced into it at each feeding.

I never have lived with a cat that liked ground meat, but a good many people have told me their cats preferred it that way. In either case the nourishment is the same. I do think, though, that cats' teeth last longer if they have hunks of meat to gnaw.

Horse. For a long time I couldn't bring myself to feed horsemeat to the cats; it just didn't seem right to eat man's noble friend. I still don't like the idea when I permit myself to think of it, but there's no doubt that horsemeat is good, nourishing and cheap. Horsemeat has the same food value as beef, except it is deficient in fat, so a teaspoonful of suet, butter or some other edible fat or oil should be added to every feeding.

Lamb and mutton. Lamb and mutton are very good cat food. Mutton is so cheap I wonder more people don't buy it for cats.

Cats have a lovely time with breast of lamb; the bones don't splinter and cats like to chew out all the cartilaginous connective tissue, which is full of good, healthy, bone-building calcium.

Veal. Many people believe that veal is unfit food for cats; to hear them talk you'd think it was practically poisonous. That the cow should be the staff of life to cats, and the little calf a menace, doesn't make sense. Belief in the dangerousness of veal originated in prerefrigerator days when veal was fairly risky food for anyone because it spoiled quickly. Nowadays veal is as safe as beef or lamb. Cats like it.

Pork. Pork is the last meat for cats. Raw pork, no matter how carefully it is inspected by American methods, may contain the larvae of trichinae. Trichinae are worms, microscopic at some stages, which settle between the muscular folds in humans and animals and cause trichinosis. No cure for trichinosis has been developed, and any person or animal that eats raw pork and gets trichinosis is lucky if he lives to regret it. Thorough cooking absolutely destroys trichinae, and pork for any use must be cooked done before it is safe to eat. This includes the innards.

Ham and bacon should never be fed to a cat. Smoked, corned or salted meat may make a cat ill.

EGGS

If you would have a cat with shining fur, feed it eggs two or three times a week. An egg is a whole chicken in the making; it contains everything needed to build a healthy animal. Eggs deserve an important share of the credit for Pickle's long life.

Raw eggs are best. Soft-boiled, poached or scrambled eggs are good. Fried eggs are greasy and slow to be digested. Hard-boiled eggs are constipating. Eggs, eggs and eggs may cause diarrhea.

Sick cats or old cats should have just the yolk beaten with milk, as the white of the egg is not so easily digested.

The only thing wrong with eggs is that they don't put sods on the dyke, as they say in Holland. Give a cat two eggs, which will nourish it until tomorrow, and within two hours that cat will swear by Bubastis that it hasn't eaten for a week. Sensible people will ignore such protestations; others, including me, give the cat anything to shut it up. This may be your chance to work off some of that canned cat food you got stuck with.

FISH

Everyone knows that cats like fish. Any sort of fish or crustacean is good for cats, provided it is fresh enough for you to eat. Spoiled fish will kill a cat.

Fish absolutely must be cooked. Fish and pork are the two inviolable exceptions to the rule that it's foolish to cook for a cat. Tapeworms in one of their complicated larval stages live in fish, and feeding raw fish to a cat simply invites tapeworm.

You must bone the cat's fish. Cats mustn't have fish bones ever, not big ones, or little ones, or sort of soft ones, or any other kind of fish bones. A fish bone may stick in the cat's throat and choke it. A swallowed fish bone may puncture the stomach wall. A cat's stomach contains enough hydrochloric acid to dissolve any bone eventually. Unfortunately bones don't wait to be dissolved. If your cat has had fish bones and survived that was pure accident and may not happen again.

For a cat that goes outdoors, fish is fine as often as you are willing to cook and bone it. If the cat can't go out, don't feed it fish too often. It is hard to live in an apartment with a cat that has had fish every day for a week; the whole place smells like a fish market at low tide. Fish once in a while will please the cat and won't bother you.

POULTRY AND GAME

This may seem like a very fancy heading for a paragraph on cat food. It isn't really. Even city cats can have chicken gizzards and hearts and heads. Once in a while rabbits can be bought at cat-food prices, and how cats love them!

The butcher will give you chicken heads if you ask, whether you're buying chicken or not. If you can stand the sight of them they make good cat food. Chicken heads are the exception to the rule that cats mustn't have poultry bones; the head bones don't splinter. You give them to the cat just so, no cooking. Squeamish people needn't even unwrap the parcel, just put it down and run.

Rabbit must be cooked. Cats are not subject to tularemia but they can get dog tapeworm from eating raw rabbit.

Poultry bones are as dangerous as fish bones. If you had ever seen the misery of a cat with a bone in its throat, or the slow, agonizing death of a cat that had its stomach wall punctured, you would never let any cat friend of yours within a mile of a sharp bone.

PREPARED FOODS

The prepared foods that come in cans or jars or paper containers may be nourishing and some cats may like them—mine don't. There's nothing wrong with these concoctions, you understand; but there just isn't enough right with them to interest a pampered cat. If you should find a prepared food that the cat likes, by all means keep some on hand as an emergency ration. As I have said before and shall say again, no one thing should be fed day after day without change.

Canned fish is fine for a change. Take the bones out.

Some cats like a little snack of dog biscuit or dehydrated cat food, and it seems to agree with them. Such things are about as much kin to food as the canapés at a cocktail party are to dinner.

PÂTÉS DE LA MAISON

Some people simply love to cook for cats and this book won't stop them. One of my best friends cooks for her cats. Mary prepares this recipe in quantity and doles it out as needed to Oscar, Oscar's daughter Mittsy, and her son Rinso. All three are in beautiful condition, so if you're dead set on cooking for cats you might as well have a good recipe:

Pâté Oscar

1 lb. lung, boiled in very little water
1 lb. fish, boiled separately, also in very little water, and carefully boned.
2 cups crumbled dog food.
½ cup tomato juice
1 teaspoon cod liver oil
Grind the cooked fish and lung together. Pour the liquid the fish was cooked in over the dog food, mix and let cool. Combine the ground lung, fish and dog food, add the tomato juice and cod liver oil. Pack in jars and keep in the refrigerator until used.

This recipe may be varied indefinitely. You could substitute dry toast for the dog biscuit. You could use kidney, liver, heart, shrimp, brains, or chicken gizzards in place of the lungs or fish or both.

BONES

Cats are not very efficient bone gnawers. Most cats pick at a big bone and leave it. I never knew a cat that didn't love

dangerous little bones. Large beef or veal bones are safe because
they don't splinter even if the cat bites pieces off. Bones from
the breast and neck of lamb are safe. Leg of lamb bones are
safe and uninteresting to cats. Lamb chop bones are risky and
alluring; cooked chop bones splinter and raw ones may splinter.
All other bones are potentially deadly.

VEGETABLES

Vegetables should be fed to cats in doses, not in portions.

The following vegetables usually agree with cats, and most
cats will eat some of them:

Boiled string beans, asparagus, onions, leeks, green peas, carrots. Also grated raw carrots, broccoli, tomatoes, lettuce, celery,
parsley, chickory, endive, chives, spinach, corn salad, and mus-
tard greens.

Cats must never have starchy, greasy, or highly seasoned vegetables.

A few cats like fruit, particularly grapes, oranges and berries.

A grown cat should have half a clove of garlic mashed into its
food about every two weeks as worm insurance.

TABLE SCRAPS

Plate scrapings are an inglorious medley at best: fat, bones,
congealed grease, gravy, potatoes, and over-seasoned vegetables; everything a cat shouldn't have.

Also, it is practically impossible to feed a cat table scraps and
stay friends with your family. Cats don't regard table scraps as
food, and consequently they drag bones and fat around the
floor like make-believe mice and leave them in strategic places
for people to slip on or turn an ankle.

If throwing away table scraps makes you feel wasteful, get
some chickens.

LIQUID REFRESHMENT

Cats must always have access to clean, fresh water.

Some people think that if cats drink milk they don't need water. Others say they never saw a cat drink water, so why put water out for the cat? Cats do drink water. House cats that are deprived of water soon learn to drink from the toilet or the aquarium. Some cats prefer the toilet or the aquarium after a while. It's a bit nicer to give the cat its own waterbowl.

Whether they drink milk or don't drink milk, cats absolutely must have water. Cats need water more than most animals because they wash so assiduously. The fact that cats dislike the clammy feel of wet fur does not mean that they never get thirsty.

Milk is all right for kittens and somewhat overrated as food for adult cats. Some cats are exceedingly fond of milk. Some cats are indifferent to milk. Milk disagrees with some cats. Some cats like milk even though it makes them sick. Some cats don't like milk. Find out which group your cat belongs to and use your judgment.

A cup of milk with an egg beaten into it is nourishing and satisfying, if it agrees with the cat.

Cream makes cats fat and unsightly; you know there's no Charm School for cats.

TEMPERATURE

When you feed the cat always make sure the food is about room temperature. This is as important as the right kind of food and plenty of water.

If the food is hot, wait until it cools, no matter how the cat clamors. To give a hungry cat hot food is really unkind.

Cold food can kill a cat. If the cat thinks it's starving, you know better, so let Puss wait until the food warms, or you warm it over a pan of hot water.

Cold milk is just as bad as cold meat, worse, maybe, because cats drink faster than they eat. Hundreds of kittens are killed every summer by people who play with them until they're hot and tired, and then pour kitty a nice big bowl of milk right out of the ice box. People kill themselves the same way, but they really haven't any business doing it to kittens.

HOW MUCH FOOD?

Some cats look like scarecrows on less than half a pound of meat a day. Some cats thrive on next to nothing. Only the cat you live with can tell you how much food it needs to stay in good condition. If a new cat comes your way, take a quarter of a pound of meat a day as the basic ration, and work up or down from there.

A quarter of a pound of lean beef, lamb, mutton, or veal, liver, kidney, or heart will about equal six ounces of brains, lungs, or boneless fish, or two large eggs.

HOW OFTEN

A grown cat needs one meal a day, not breakfast, lunch, dinner, and a snack in between. Possibly one cat in a million needs breakfast because it doesn't eat enough dinner to keep in good condition; your cat isn't likely to be the millionth one, and I'm not going to tell you how to sin.

DIETARY DON'TS

I know this is repetitious, but cats simply must not have: raw fish, raw pork, fish bones or fish with the bones left in, poultry bones or any other small bones, ham, bacon, corned beef, sausages, bread, potatoes, cake, pie, spaghetti, macaroni, noodles, baked beans, any other kind of dried beans or peas, fresh lima beans, turnips, parsnips, the cabbage family (including sauerkraut and excepting broccoli), corn, alligator pears, bananas, porridge, coffee, tea, cocoa, cocktails, candy, popcorn, peanuts, or cheese.

Anything not mentioned in this chapter as suitable cat food, whether listed above or not, should be strictly avoided.

No hot food. No cold food. No highly seasoned food.

If you stick to the rules you'll have a healthy cat.

IF THE CAT WON'T EAT

If the cat refuses food which you consider perfectly good cat food, take the dish away and let the cat wait until tomorrow. Skipping a meal won't hurt a healthy cat. Coaxing a cat to eat is a waste of time. Leaving dishes of uneaten food around won't tempt the cat and will draw roaches.

If the cat refuses food two days in succession and still seems healthy, you're entitled to suspect hairballs or constipation. The treatment is the same for either.*

If the cat cries for food and then won't eat, the odds are about even that it has (a) a toothache,† or (b) a hankering for something else. Deal with the hankering your own way.

If the cat refuses food and acts sick, you rush it to the vet. Fast.

* See section on hairballs.
† See section on toothache.

VI

How to Feed a Kitten

A kitten is a baby cat, not a baby cow or a baby horse or a baby human. When a kitten is about three weeks old its first teeth begin to break through the gums, and the kitten is ready for raw meat. Anyone who is shocked at the idea never watched a cat feed kittens. A wise mamma cat starts bringing in mice as soon as her kittens' eyes open, sometimes even sooner, and the moment the kittens have any teeth at all she starts feeding them mice, and teaching them how to catch mice, which makes a mouse a sort of edible primer. A cat that lives in a mouseless apartment will share her own meat with the kittens if they aren't fed properly.

Kittens need exactly the same food as cats, except less of it and oftener. Don't you believe any sentimental nonsense about how baby kittens are unable to digest meat.

Remember that all cat food must be warmed to room temperature, and this is especially important when you're fixing kitten food.

Remember, cats of any age must always have plenty of fresh clean water.

Some people cut the cat's meat into dainty little bites. Others give their cats hunks to gnaw. Most cats enjoy gnawing hunks. Very young kittens, old cats, cats with toothache and pantywaist cats that are naturally pernickety can't, or won't, manage hunks.

To repeat:
Kittens as well as cats usually dislike the texture of ground beef.
Starchy food is bad for kittens and cats.
Never feed a kitten or a cat raw fish or raw pork.
Fish for a kitten, as well as for a cat, must be carefuly boned.
Poultry bones are absolutely deadly to kitten or cat.
Keep the kitten away from all small bones.

When raising a litter of kittens it is advisable to give each kitten its own dish. This makes it possible to keep an eye on the greedy kitten, and gives the slow one a chance.

Weaning a kitten is dealt with elsewhere.*

The following chart is designed to show you how to feed a kitten from the time it is about six weeks old until at the age of six months it becomes dietetically a cat. In case you don't know how old your kitten is, you can make a pretty good guess by examining its teeth. A kitten six weeks old has a full set of small, sharp teeth. When the kitten is between five and seven months old the milk teeth are replaced by permanent teeth, and the kitten is a cat.

*See chapter: How to Raise Kittens from Scratch.

SIX WEEKS TO THREE MONTHS

SIX MEALS A DAY

Breakfast.   2 tablespoonfuls of milk-and-egg mixture warmed to room temperature.

To make this you pour the contents of a tall can of *unsweetened* evaporated milk, or a pint of homogenized milk, into a jar, add one slightly beaten egg and shake until thoroughly mixed. Keep this mixture in the refrigerator and warm each portion before feeding it to the kitten.

Midmorning. 1 tablespoonful of lean, raw beef cut fine, not ground,

or

1 tablespoonful of raw beef, veal, or lamb kidney cut fine.

Lunchtime.   2 tablespoonfuls of milk and egg mixture.

Teatime.   1 tablespoonful of minced raw meat.

Dinnertime.   2 tablespoonfuls of milk and egg mixture.

Bedtime.   1 tablespoonful of minced raw meat.

Once a week mash half a clove of garlic in the kitten's food to prevent worms. Kittens are more subject to worms * than cats are, and so they should be garlicked oftener. Garlic really does remove ordinary round worms, which commonly attack kittens. It is the only vermifuge which may safely be given to a kitten at home. It won't hurt the kitten if it hasn't got worms. If the kitten smells a bit garlicky for a few hours, that's a small price to pay for wormlessness. Besides, you could have spaghetti the same day and then you wouldn't notice. You mash the garlic with a fork or spoon, and wash up as soon as the kitten has

* See discussion of worms.

eaten, first with cold water, then with hot and soapy. Don't let the thought of garlic scare you—the pyramids were built by garlic eaters. When the symptoms of worms disappear, it is safe to suppose that the worms are gone.

If you adhere faithfully to this schedule your kitten's strength will be as the strength of ten. Scientists have calculated that a hundred and fifty kittens are as strong as a man. I'll bet the scientist who worked that out never raised a kitten, for one healthy kitten can wear out the strongest man in about ten minutes by scampering up and down him, slapping his nose, nibbling his ears, and swinging on his tie.

Be sure the kitten gets meat at bedtime; meat sticks to the ribs best. Also, meat at night won't send the kitten in search of his pan, as the milk mixture will.

Toward the end of this period increase the meat little by little until by the time the kitten is three months old you are feeding it about half as much again.

Always have fresh clean water where the kitten can reach it. (I don't mean to nag—some people don't realize how important it is.)

THREE TO FOUR MONTHS

FIVE MEALS A DAY

At three months a kitten is all legs and ears, and you wonder how you ever thought this was going to be a handsome cat. About now a kitten discovers the desirability of washing its face and develops a passionate desire to sharpen its claws on the best furniture. It might catch a mouse.

Breakfast.   A quarter of a cup of milk and egg mixture, warmed to room temperature, of course.

Midmorning. Two tablespoonfuls of lean, raw beef, lamb, or mutton, or half a lamb kidney.

Midafternoon. A quarter of a cup of milk and egg.

Dinnertime. Two tablespoonfuls of raw meat or cooked fish carefully boned, with a few string beans, or a spoonful of shredded spinach or lettuce. Not more than one teaspoonful of vegetable.

Bedtime. Two tablespoonfuls of meat or cooked fish.

Continue half a clove of garlic once a week.

FOUR TO FIVE MONTHS

FOUR MEALS A DAY

Now you can vary the kitten's diet by feeding heart, liver, lungs, brains, and kidneys as often as plain beef or lamb. Continue feeding garlic once a week.

Discontinue the midafternoon milk feeding.

Double the quantity of milk and egg mixture in the morning.

Move the midmorning feeding up to lunchtime.

Breakfast. A third to a half cup of milk and egg mixture.

Lunchtime. Two tablespoonfuls of lean, raw meat or innards.

Dinnertime. Four tablespoonfuls of meat or cooked, boned fish mixed with a teaspoonful of any recommended vegetable.

Bedtime. Two tablespoonfuls of meat. No vegetables at bedtime.

FIVE TO SIX MONTHS

THREE MEALS A DAY

When the kitten is five months old discontinue the bedtime snack, or, if more convenient, discontinue lunch. In either case add that amount of food to the kitten's dinner. Continue feeding garlic once a week.

The kitten should have at least six ounces of solid meat or half a pound of fish or lungs or brains every day, and may need even more. It isn't just sustaining itself, it's making a big cat and burning up energy like mad.

After a kitten is six months old you feed it as if it were a cat. It may not become a cat the day it's six months old, a kitten becomes a cat when it feels like it, but from here on it eats like a cat.

A cat should have one meal a day and milk, if milk agrees with it.

And of course, always, plenty of water.

VII

How to Raise Kittens from Scratch

This is not a job that any right-minded person would undertake for fun. Perhaps it's a job no right-minded person would ever undertake. Yet it has been done. Mamma cats have died in kittenbirth, or abandoned their newborn kittens, or failed to produce milk, and people have raised the kittens.

FOSTER MOTHERS

The best way to raise motherless kittens is to get them a foster mother. You may know of a cat who lost her kittens and would be delighted to raise your orphans; the animal welfare society might have a recently kittenless mother cat for you, or even a bitch who has lost her puppies; an ad in the paper might fetch a wet nurse. In any case, a foster mother must be obtained quickly because your kittens won't last long without food. And she must be introduced to your kittens before her milk dries up and she loses interest in anybody's offspring. Be sure she is healthy and amiable.

If you get a foster mother, make her comfortable, then gently squeeze out a little of her milk, smear it on the kittens and present them to her as quietly as possible. Don't have the family and the neighbors in to watch; they'll only make her nervous. If she accepts the kittens, all you need do is read the next chapter,* and proceed accordingly.

WHAT TO DO IF YOU CAN'T GET A FOSTER MOTHER
(ARE YOU THAT ANXIOUS TO RAISE KITTENS?)

If you fail to find a nurse-cat, or a bitch, within twenty-four hours you must decide whether to raise the kittens, or not. Being a foster mamma cat is an arduous job and nobody will blame you if you don't attempt it. You'll blame yourself if you try and then give up.

Before deciding to become a kitten nurse you should consider the following: Can you stick as close to those kittens as their own mother would? This means feeding them every two hours, day and night, for a week, and almost as often for two weeks longer. Are you that anxious to raise kittens? Newborn kittens are little more than embryos; they know only warmth and cold, repletion and hunger, comfort and discomfort, so wouldn't it be better to let the vet snuff them out quickly? No? Well, you asked for it.

* See chapter: How to Help a Cat Raise Kittens.

THE KITTENS' BOX

First, and quickly, you get the kittens a box. Cardboard boxes from the grocery, easy to get and easy to throw away, are as good as anything. If you have only one or two kittens get a small box, a shoe box will do. Three or four kittens need a box about twice the size of a shoe box.

Fold several layers of newspaper in the bottom of the box as leak insurance. Line the box with flannel, which is soft, warm, and easily washed. If you don't intend to wash blankets for kittens, I hope you've got a whale of a lot of old rags around because the kittens' bedding must be changed every day if they haven't any mamma to clean up after them. If you haven't any flannel and can't get any, use wool, part wool or soft old towels, not bath towels. Do not use silk, rayon, old stockings, stiff or starched cloth, or any very sheer material that the kittens can snarl themselves in. The idea is to keep them as cosy as their mother would. The sides as well as the bottom of the box should be lined. This is easily done by bringing the cloth over the edges of the box and sticking it to the outside with adhesive tape or scotch tape.

WARMTH

In warm weather the kittens will keep warm without additional heat. If the weather is cool you'll have to provide auxiliary heat equal to a mamma cat. The best thing is an electric heating pad that gets just so warm and no warmer when set on "Low." The heating pad should be suspended so that it comes down all one side of the box to the bottom, without dragging; you can tack the outside cover of the pad to the wall behind

Are you really that anxious to raise kittens?

the box—don't stick tacks in the heating element. Lacking a heating pad, you can use a hot-water bottle, well wrapped in flannel. If you use a hot-water bottle you'll need a larger box. Set the hot-water bottle up along the side of the box, as directed for a heating pad, so the kittens can cuddle up to it as if it were a mamma cat. Make sure that bottle or pad can't fall over on the kittens and smother them. Now the box is ready for the kittens, until tomorrow morning when you'll have to make it up all over again.

FOOD

You need one, or preferably two, doll nursing bottles; with two extra rubber nipples; with two bottles you can feed two kittens at once and save some time. If you can't get doll nursing bottles, get baby bottles with the smallest possible nipples, though they may be too large for newborn kittens. A third possibility is what southern mammies call a sugar-tit; this is a scrap of non-raveling white cloth, such as an old handkerchief, twisted to something of a point and dipped first in milk and then in the kitten's mouth. It is possible to feed several kittens simultaneously by using sugar-tits. Their only disadvantage is drippiness. Naturally, sugar-tits for kittens are not sweetened—sweetening is for babies. Whatever you use must be sterilized before each using.

Next you lay in a hefty stack of reading matter and check up on the alarm clock; the kittens must be fed every two hours, twelve times a day, all through the night.

There are two schools of thought on kitten feeding: The pinch-of-this-and-dab-of-that-to-make-it-scientific school, and the copy-cat school. I belong to the copy-cat school because I think cats make the best possible food for kittens; at any rate, cats have been thriving on it for some fifty million years. Lacking cat's milk, kittens must have the next best thing, which fresh cow's milk is not. Cow's milk is watery stuff at best, intended to fill up a calf, not a kitten. Also, cow's milk contains considerable sugar and little fat. Cat's milk is just the reverse, it has little sugar, a lot of fat, and is concentrated nourishment for small kittens.

Goat's milk is the best substitute for cat's milk. Canned goat's milk can be bought in almost any drug store.

There is also a synthetic bitch's milk that can be had in many drug stores. It is called "Esbilac," and is an excellent substitute for cat's milk.

The canned goat's milk and Esbilac are far and away the best foods for motherless kittens, but if you can't get either, then canned, unsweetened, evaporated milk, preferably irradiated, may also be used. Many, many kittens have been raised on it. Evaporated milk is cheap, good and easily obtained. Don't confuse it with sweetened condensed milk, which is often given to human babies. I mean *unsweetened, evaporated milk*.

Goat's milk or Esbilac should be fed according to the directions on the container.

You feed the evaporated milk straight, just as it comes from the can, not diluted with anything, warmed to 100 degrees Fahrenheit.

Allow a tablespoonful of milk per kitten at each feeding, and watch them carefully. If one kitten seems to fall behind the average, give it a little extra. If the kittens want more than a tablespoonful, give it to them.

After each feeding stroke the kittens' bellies with a firm, very gentle, downward motion. Every mamma cat does this after the kittens have suckled. She washes them all over and then licks their tummies thoroughly so the gentle massage will promote digestion and elimination. You don't have to wash them all over, you shouldn't wash them at all, but rubbing is just as important as proper feeding. The kittens' bowels should move after each feeding.

You keep this up, every two hours, night and day, for a week. In your spare time you sterilize nursing bottles.

On the eighth day you make two changes: (1) You add an egg to their food: empty a large can of evaporated milk into a glass jar, add one egg and shake well. During the daytime, feed them milk and egg. At night continue feeding plain milk. The food should always be warmed to 100° F. (2) You feed the kittens every three hours at night, instead of every two hours. Nice, eh?

THE KITTENS' EYES

Between the eighth and the twelfth day the kittens will begin to open their eyes. The first day or so they can't really see, so don't expect them to.

From the time the kittens are born until they begin to walk, their eyes must be protected from bright light. This is true before their eyes begin to open, as well as during the period when they are starting to see. You can take them into daylight to look at them, of course, but *not* into direct sunshine, and *not* near an unshaded electric light. The rest of the time they should be kept in a dim light.

As the kittens grow, give them a slightly larger box, big enough to wiggle in and not large enough to get lost in.

After the kittens are two weeks old you can begin spreading the daytime feedings little by little until one feeding has been eliminated. Also increase the quantity of food very slightly. Here you must use your judgment; the kittens should grow steadily and evenly.

By the time the kittens are three weeks old, their eyes are open wide, they're beginning to toddle and tussle, and their teeth are starting to break through the gums.

THE FIRST MEAT

Now teeth are made to eat with; cats know it and kittens know it. For some strange reason, or lack of reason, a lot of people persist in continuing to feed milk to kittens that are ready to chew the hind leg off a cow. Others acknowledge that teeth are made to chew with, and cook up a mess of porridge for the kittens, which is almost the worst thing they could eat. Did you ever hear of a mamma cat going out and catching a bowl of mush for her kittens? The day the kittens are three weeks old, whether they're orphans or not, they should have raw meat.

Buy a piece of lean beef, preferably round steak for this because it contains less fiber than other cuts. Trim off all the fat. Scrape across the grain of the meat with a dull knife. What comes off will be nothing much, and that's what you give the kittens. The meat must be scraped, not ground, because scraped meat contains all the good and very little fiber.

Roll the scrapings into dabs about the size of dried beans. Warm them in your hand or roll them on a warm saucer to take the chill off; don't have the saucer warm enough to turn the meat gray—that's cooking. Make two dabs for each kitten.

Hold a dab under a kitten's nose and watch it vanish! If there's a reactionary in the lot, let that one watch until the others have finished. If it still refuses, put a crumb of meat gently into its mouth; a lot of reactionaries don't know what's good for them until it's shoved into their mouths. After the first taste of meat your problem will be to keep the kittens from eating your fingers.

The first day, those little dabs of meat are just extras. The second day, increase the amount of meat, prepared the same way, to about half a teaspoonful for each kitten and substitute it for one milk feeding. The third day, substitute a teaspoonful of meat for the milk-and-egg mixture first thing in the morning and last feeding before you go to bed. If the kittens don't wake you up that night, you needn't get up and feed them.

Gradually increase the food until each kitten has a heaping teaspoonful of meat morning and night. Also increase the milk-and-egg mixture to two tablespoonfuls per kitten.

WEANING

By the middle of the third week, the kittens should be drinking and eating out of a dish and you merely referee the scrimmage. If the kittens don't learn to lap of their own accord, dip a finger in the milk and let them lick; while they're licking, lower the finger into the milk and they'll lap before they know it, and then they're weaned.

The kittens should have seven or eight meals a day until they're six weeks old.*

* See also chapters: How to Feed a Kitten; How to Feed a Cat.

VIII

How to Help a Cat Raise Kittens

PLANNED KITTENS

People who keep she-cats should expect to raise kittens. It's a cat's destiny and her pleasure. The only exceptions are ailing, runty, undernourished, malformed, rickety, very old or very young cats—Siamese sometimes come in heat before they are five months old, and of course that won't do. No cat should be bred before it is a year old. Some of these conditions can be corrected; youth, of course, corrects itself; ailments or poor feeding may possibly be corrected. Malformations and rickets cannot be corrected entirely, even with good care, and cats with such afflictions should not be bred. The trouble is that there are a few people who can see no flaw in their darlings; they rush out and breed cats that are not physically fit to bear kittens, and when the cats have difficulty giving birth to their kittens these impetuous folk never consider that it might be their fault, but instead blame everybody from the neighbors to the King of Siam. Fortunately this brand of fool is rare, though noisy.

If you have the least doubt about the physical perfection of your cat, take her to the veterinarian *before you breed her,* and ask whether she is in suitable condition to bear kittens. Even if you haven't any doubt, there's no harm in asking. Bad teeth, for example, may make it impossible for a cat to cut the umbilical cords, which is no great problem if you are on hand to do it for her, but could cause trouble if the cat is alone, or if you don't know how to cut the cord properly.

The next step, if the cat cost money and possibly if she didn't, is to arrange a marriage of convenience with some eugenically suitable tom. The ins and outs of cat breeding are baffling to an amateur and complicated to anyone, so I think the choice of a mate might well be left to an authority on the subject. Except for one point: make sure you like the tomcat who will sire the kittens, that he is pleasant and intelligent as well as suitably handsome. There's no possible point in having an undesirable cat-in-law in the family. Even if you don't have to put up with him around the house, his offspring will be all over the place.

THE CAT'S CHOICE

Plain cats, and any fancy ones that can manage it, go out and pick their own mates and start their own kittens. This method, haphazard though it is and unpredictable in result, has been followed by cats and humans since time began. When the cat goes out, it is safe to assume that she'll come home with kittens on the way.

FEEDING THE PREGNANT CAT

This doesn't mean you have to get excited. Cats take kittens as they come and there's little need for people to do more. When the cat begins to bulge convincingly, usually around the fifth or sixth week, it is advisable to increase her food a little, particularly the milk, if milk agrees with her, and the eggs and meat. The period of gestation is theoretically sixty-three days—nine weeks. Actually, it may vary from fifty-nine days to sixty-four. Young cats are likelier to have their kittens early, and old cats late. The most important precaution is the avoidance of constipation. For this you mix a teaspoonful of olive oil or other pure vegetable salad oil in the cat's food every other day. If she shows symptoms of constipation, give her a teaspoonful of salad oil every day.

Don't encourage a pregnant cat to jump or play wildly. On the other hand, don't coop her up so she can't get any exercise.

By the time her teats begin to swell kittens aren't far off. At this point nice people fix a special bed for the accouchement, something pretty grand in the way of a cat's cradle. No doubt cats appreciate these little attentions, but they usually have their kittens in the hayloft or a dresser drawer or the middle of your bed.

WHAT TO DO WHEN THE KITTENS ARE BORN

If the cat is healthy, not deformed in any way, and has good teeth she should have kittens easily and without help. A sickly or malformed cat should not be allowed to breed. If the cat's teeth are bad you may be needed to cut the umbilical cord. Use sterilized scissors and cut about an inch away from the kitten's belly. The cord should not bleed; if it does, tie a soft cord around it for an hour or so. Don't interfere at all if you can possibly avoid it. Cats know how to have kittens and meddling only makes them nervous.

Each kitten comes in a separate package, covered by a thin membrane like a cellophane wrapper, usually with a gelatinous afterbirth attached. The cat eats the membrane and the afterbirth, which may be expelled considerably later. This is perfectly all right and it is good for the cat.

Unless some complication develops, there is no need to send for the vet. If the cat labors more than three or four hours, or seems unable to get a kitten born, or bleeds unduly, or seems really ill, by all means get the vet fast. But remember that there is very little chance of any complication.

Once the kittens are born, you may be able to persuade the cat to move into that nice box you fixed, if she considers it suitable.

The box should be long enough for the mamma cat to stretch out full length without bumping, and wide enough for the kittens to roll around a little. If the box is too small the cat may lie on the kittens and smother them. If it is too large the kittens may get lost and miss enough meals to stunt their growth.

Line the box with flannel or some other soft, firmly woven, washable material. Keep it in a secluded, dimly lit place. And don't handle the kittens any more than necessary. Also, don't be endlessly fussing over the cat.

Make sure the cat has milk by pressing her teats very gently between thumb and forefinger, and if a droplet of milk appears it's all right. Watch the kittens until each one has suckled.

If the cat fails to produce milk within five or six hours—this doesn't happen often—send for the vet.

HOW TO DESTROY UNWANTED KITTENS

It sometimes happens that the kittens simply can't be kept, or that only one kitten can properly be taken care of and kept to old age. If you can't keep the kittens, the kindest way is to kill them, or have the S.P.C.A. do so, as soon as they are born—they're scarcely more than embryos then, and the mother cat will forget them in a few hours.

Killing kittens is an unhappy task at best, but the quickest way is the kindest. Gas, chloroform, and water are about equally quick. The kittens can be placed in a perforated box and the box put in the oven with the gas turned on and not lit for a few minutes—keep the windows wide open so you don't get gassed or blow the house up. Exhaust gas from a car can be used, if a hose attached to the exhaust is run into a closed container with the kittens, and the motor kept going for three or four minutes. A wad of cotton saturated with chloroform or ether may be put in a closed box with the kittens. In any case, the box should be as small as possible. Or the kittens may be placed in a pail of tepid water and another pail set down on top of that one, so they can't swim and will drown fast. The kittens must not under any circumstances be disposed of until they are completely dead. You'd worry forever after if you thought they might have revived underground or on a garbage wagon.

And in the name of human decency, don't keep the kittens until they are days, or even weeks, old and then kill them. This is cruel to the kittens and utter wretchedness for the cat. A cat knows when her kittens should be weaned, and if they disappear sooner she goes searching and wailing and grieving to break her heart. If by the time the kittens are weaned you still haven't found really good homes for them, then you must send for the S.P.C.A.

CARE OF THE MOTHER CAT AFTER HER KITTENS HAVE BEEN KILLED

If all the kittens are taken away at birth the mother cat's milk will soon disappear, if you massage her teats three times a day with warm camphorated oil, first gently pressing the milk out.

HOW TO FEED A NURSING CAT

While she is nursing, the cat should have the same food she always had, a little more of it, and that divided into three meals a day instead of one. When the kittens are three weeks old begin tapering off very slowly, so that by the time they are weaned the mother cat is back to normal.

A well-fed cat should remain sleek and thrifty throughout pregnancy and nursing.

WHEN TO START FEEDING THE KITTENS

The day the kittens are three weeks old, you begin feeding them scraped raw beef, as directed.*

* See chapter: How to Raise Kittens from Scratch.

IX

On Caring for a Cat

HOW TO TEACH A CAT THE FUNDAMENTALS OF SOCIAL HYGIENE

Cats keep themselves clean and they have clean habits. Mamma cats housetrain their kittens while weaning them, and you can be practically certain that any kitten you buy or otherwise acquire after it has reached the ripe old age of six weeks knows the fundamentals of social hygiene. It knows that, like all cats the world around, it must dig deep, wide, and handsome to conceal this evidence of its presence from roving enemies, or it must hide the evidence in some other, more ingenious manner. If you and the cat see eye to eye in the matter of privacy, all's well. If not, you'll have to find out what the cat wants and provide same.

Ordinarily, housebreaking a cat is no trouble at all. If the new cat is half grown or older, you simply make it feel at home with you, feed it, let it out in the yard and watch until you're sure the cat knows what yards are for. Call it in, and dismiss hygienic considerations from your mind. Next time the cat wants out it will tell you.

A little kitten is better trained to a pan at first, even if there's a yard. You might not be around when it wants out (which is about twenty times a day when they're little), or it might forget where the door is. In either case the kitten is likely to make sanitary arrangements indoors that wouldn't coincide with your ideas.

The location of the kitten's pan is important; you can't expect a small kitten to travel great distances in search of a comfort station. Neither can you put the pan in a different place every day and expect the kitten to guess where you hid it. The pan must be kept in one place, even though it inconveniences you, until the kitten grows up enough to cope with the vagaries of human nature.

Any large, shallow pan that doesn't leak and can't rust will do. A cheap, enameled dishpan is fine for cats. A kitten needs a shallower pan, so it can see over the edge; cats don't like to jump blindly into cat pans.

What to put in the cat's pan is debatable. Some people use sand, but sand gets tracked around the house, scratches the floor and cuts the rugs. Also, disposing of used cat-sand is a problem for people who live in apartments. Shredded paper doesn't get tracked around; on the other hand it is neither very absorbent nor easily disposed of. If you put flat paper in the cat's pan the cat will shred it. I have found sawdust more satisfactory than anything. Sawdust can be obtained at any lumber yard or from the butcher. Ten cents worth lasts about a month. Sawdust is exceedingly absorbent, and pine sawdust out-smells cat for at least twelve hours. If it is handled with care, sawdust will not stop up the drain, which is a great advantage. The sawdust particles that get tracked around the house won't scratch floors or cut rugs and are easily swept up.

If you know you're going to get a cat, have its pan ready when it arrives. If the cat comes unexpectedly, fix its pan first thing. Show it to the cat at once. Then, as soon as you've fed the cat take it to the pan again. Keep it there until it uses the pan. Don't clean the pan until it has been used a second time. Whatever you do, don't clean the cat's pan with carbolic acid or any other coal tar derivative. Wash the pan twice a day with soap and water and a long-handled brush and it won't need any other cleaning.

A woman I know bought a full-grown çat and a proper cat pan. Then she scalded the pan with carbolic acid solution, laid in it a folded newspaper, and expected the cat to use it. Even the odor of carbolic will make a cat ill, so naturally the cat didn't use its pan. A day passed, two days, three days, and the cat did nothing at all. The fourth evening she came home to find that the cat had sprinkled on each of the twenty-four buttons that tufted her daybed, messed in the wastebasket and left by way of the fire escape.

If the cat won't use its pan there's a reason. The location of the pan may be so public as to offend the cat's sense of modesty. The cat may have been educated differently; cats that have lived with writers, for example, are usually trained to some other cover material than paper, lest they get disrespectful notions about manuscripts. I used to know a cat that had been found in a disreputable alley and would not use a cat pan. He used wastebaskets and the garbage can and once he used a guest's top hat. His distracted folks finally decided he'd learned his manners in an ash can. They got him an ash can and he used it.

Some cats think they know more about comfort stations than people do, and take a fancy to the bath tub or the shower or the fireplace. I suppose the bath tub and shower fanciers are civilized cats who appreciate modern conveniences and resent efforts to impose primitive sanitation on them. Anyhow, they're usually stubborn. You might try keeping the bathroom door closed, if you can remember to close it, and if you can find a place outside the bathroom for the cat's pan. An inch of water in the bathtub and an inch in the wash basin might drive the cat to use the toilet, and then you'd have something to brag about.

One of my friends who had a pet wildcat, a real bobcat, invented an improved cat pan that some other cats might like. This was a large white enameled pan, into the bottom of which she fitted a broiler rack made of fairly close, heavy mesh. Over this she put two or three large paper towels, and when the pan had been used she simply dropped the paper towels down the toilet and rinsed the pan with warm water. She kept a film of water in the bottom of the pan, with a scattering of soap flakes on the surface. The pan never smelled and was awfully easy to keep clean. Eventually the wildcat learned to use the toilet.

The fireplace habit is hardest to cure. Cats that can go out may prefer the fireplace. You may break this up by putting some used ashes from the fireplace in the cat's pan just this once. Then scrub the fireplace with soap and water, dust it thoroughly with the powder that is supposed to keep cats off the furniture, barricade the fireplace, and cross your fingers. If you keep the fireplace barricaded long enough the cat will have to use its pan. Once it starts using its pan the fireplace is safe.

If a cat that has been housetrained suddenly ceases to be, and you haven't been hiding its pan or messing around with smelly disinfectants, the cat is probably sick.

If the cat suddenly begins sprinkling a little here and a little there it has sex on its mind. This problem, which has nothing

Barricade the fireplace and cross your fingers

to do with sanitation, is deliberate advertising in defiance of caution, roving enemies, or punishment.*

HOW TO GROOM A CAT

BATHE OR BRUSH?

The Chinese are said to have a cat-washing day once a year. That's once a year too often to please a cat. Washing cats, even white ones, is a bad habit to get into; cat fur wasn't meant to be washed. Soap dries out the natural oils in the cat's fur and sometimes sets up skin irritations, so in the long run you spoil the cat's coat instead of improving it. A cat should be washed only if it has a skin condition that can be cured by bathing, or if it is so dirty that it doesn't know where to start washing itself. Washing is not a substitute for brushing.

HOW TO WASH A CAT

The best way I've found to bathe a cat, when it must be done, is to use the bathtub with a rubber skid mat in the bottom or a bath mat that the cat can sink its claws in and feel secure. The water should not come above the cat's neck. Use tepid water and pure neutral soap. *Never* wash a cat with medicated soap of any kind. Soap the cat all over thoroughly, being careful not to get soap in its eyes, and rinse off with a hand spray. Wrap the cat in a bath towel and rub it as dry as possible. Keep the cat in a warm, draftless room until you know it is thoroughly dry. If you wash the cat at night keep it indoors until morning.

HOW TO BRUSH A CAT

A bath, remember, is emergency treatment. Brushing is every-day grooming. The best cat brush I ever had was a little round rubber disc with rubber projections on it that had been invented

* See chapter: Dat Ole Debbil Sex.

to massage the human scalp. It really takes cat hairs off a cat and I wish somebody would manufacture a similar dingus, somewhat larger, easier to hold, and shaped to fit a cat's back rather than the human head. A good stiff bristle brush is next best. Never use a wire brush on a cat; it pulls the hair out. Cats that live in the house should be brushed every day. Long-haired cats should also be combed. Faithful brushing prevents the cat from swallowing cat hairs and getting hairballs, and it makes the cat's coat shine. It also keeps the house from being cat hairs all over.

Brushing a cat really is fun because the cat enjoys it so much. Cat brushing at my house usually turns into a game. I try to start at the head and work down the back to the tip of the tail and then turn the cat over. Actually, the cat being brushed rolls over immediately. The other cats pile in my lap and demand to be brushed too. I try to be impartial, a lick here and a swipe there and hope the cats are clean.

Some cats like to have their fur brushed the wrong way; Pickle does, for example. They are the easy ones to clean.

I've noticed that parti-colored cats need extra brushing on the dark spots, which may not show dirt so much but certainly do shed.

HOW TO HANDLE A CAT

HOW TO PICK IT UP

People shouldn't ever pick cats up by the scruff of the neck, not even tiny little baby kittens. Our hands are big and clumsy, we don't know how much pressure is necessary to clamp a kitten between thumb and forefinger—and we aren't cats. Cats carry kittens by the nape of the neck only until they're big enough to run around, and then stop. After that the kitten's body is too heavy for such treatment. Any cat more than six weeks old can be injured by having its whole weight hung from the nape of the neck—it might get an abdominal rupture —its eyes might pop out of their sockets.

The way to pick up a kitten is to slide a hand under its body and lift it all at once, with the other hand ready to rest its feet.

An older cat should be lifted by one hand under the body and the other bracing the hind feet. If only one hand is free, hold the cat parallel to your forearm and brace its body against yours, after you've tucked it into a comfortable position.

Don't carry a cat so that all four legs dangle helplessly—cats don't like to dangle.

HOW TO HOLD A CAT

When a cat jumps in your lap, stroke its back so it will sit down. If your legs are crossed, uncross them—cats don't like to sit on peaks, they're whole-lap-or-nothing creatures. Don't try to hold a cat in your lap by force.

HOW TO STROKE IT

This is a pretty primitive spot of advice, although people who haven't had much experience with cats might use a pointer or two. Cats like to be stroked with the fur, all the way down. A few cats like to have their fur mussed—about as many as there are little boys who like to be kissed—generally, it is wise to assume that cats don't like to be stroked the wrong way. Cats dearly love to be tickled behind the ears and under the chin.

COMFORT IN GENERAL

Cats like people who move slowly, speak softly, and make them comfortable. They also like people who wear flower scents, preferably with a wild thyme base.

They like people who wear flower scents

Cats do not like people whose body odor offends them. This may be imperceptible to any person and inoffensive to any creature except a cat. Bathing with certain well-known soaps will merely overlay one odor offensive to cats with another, equally objectionable to feline noses. People who don't smell good to cats can't ever get to first base and they might as well quit trying.

Making a cat feel comfortable is largely a matter of consideration, the sort of consideration we call good breeding, though it has little to do with ancestry and much to do with the heart. If you would make a cat comfortable, speak to it politely, handle it decorously, feed it copiously, and like it a lot.

THE CAT'S BED

The cat's bed may be as cheap or as expensive as you like, so long as it is comfortable and easily cleaned. A fancy cat bed or a box from the grocery will serve equally well, if snug and draughtproof. A cushion with a washable cover goes in the bed or box and that's all there is to it. There's no need for a mattress with innersprings or anything of the sort; and there's nothing against them if you like to spend your money that way. A cushion stuffed with cedar shavings tends to discourage fleas.

A cat that goes outdoors should have its bed in a cool, dry place to avoid sudden changes of temperature.

For the same reason, a cat that lives in the house and doesn't go out should sleep in a moderately warm room.

No cat should be obliged to sleep in a damp or draughty place.

If you let the cat choose, it will sleep with you, and save you the bother of fixing a bed.

COLLARS

I think city cats should wear collars. A collar shows the neighbors, the cat catcher, the A.S.P.C.A. and anyone else who looks, that this cat has a home and people and is not to be pitied or coveted.

I like the idea of collars for country cats; but in practice they seem a little risky. Besides, country cats aren't likely to be stolen; cars and dogs and traps are their enemies.

Some people object to collars for cats on the ground that they may snag on bushes or nails and hang the cats. The right collar is most unlikely to hang a cat. When we lived in the city the cats wore narrow, rather stiff dog collars, about half an inch wide, and loose enough to slip over their heads if they should snag. I like stiff collars better than those made of elastic or with elastic inserts. It is claimed that elastic collars cling so close to the cat's neck that they can't snag. Maybe. If the collar does snag and the cat struggles it can easily choke itself. When we moved to the country, I took the cats' collars off as soon as the neighbors became acquainted with them.

Never, never put a chain collar on a cat; they snag on everything.

If the name-plate on the cat's collar is engraved, have your own name and address put there. The statement that this is Snooky or François Villon is of interest only to you and the cat.

It is downright inhumane to tie a bell to the cat's collar. A bell won't stop a bird-catching cat from catching birds; only you can do that. A bell can snag on a bush or a nail and cause the cat to strangle itself or stay there, imprisoned, until it dies of starvation.

Bows are more dangerous than bells, unless every loop is snipped, and even then I wouldn't let a cat go outdoors wearing a bow. Cats that like to dress up can have their vanity and their fun in the house where people can watch them—finery isn't appropriate on a back fence anyway.

TOYS

Anything a cat plays with is a toy. I have seen kittens make up lovely games with fallen leaves or twigs, buttercups or roses. An empty spool is as much fun as a ball, and the very best toy I know is a piece of stiff paper—an empty cigarette package is perfect—tied around the middle with a string and hung from the ceiling or the top of a door where it can swing freely, barely clearing the floor. In addition to pleasing the cat immensely, this is one toy that can't cause you to turn an ankle if you step on it.

Catnip mice head the list of store toys, though they're more in the nature of a galloping cocktail than a toy pure and simple. Balls shouldn't be small enough for the cat to swallow or too large to clutch securely. Brightly colored balls are least liable to be stepped on. Don't give old golf balls to the cat—the gooey stuff in the center is said to be poisonous.

Cats love to play with string; but don't leave the cat alone with a length of twine lest it swallow the string or choke.

Rubber mice that squeak are wonderful. Mechanical toys have the same disadvantage when given to cats that they have when bought for small children—you must keep winding them all the time.

HOW TO TRAVEL WITH A CAT

AROUND THE CORNER

Once I had a neighbor who went walking every afternoon with an exceedingly superior Persian cat on a lead. They sauntered for several blocks, seemingly unaware of astonished people and outraged dogs—or anyhow too high-toned to notice. If your nerves and the cat's can stand it, you might try that method of taking a cat around a corner. But, remember, I didn't recommend it.

The best way to take a cat any place is in a cat carrier, cat basket, or other container which is ventilated, fairly comfortable, and closes securely. In an emergency an onion sack makes a pretty good satchel—if they didn't look so funny, I'd recommend them. In case of fire or accident, when there isn't even time to find an onion sack, use a pillow slip, though the cloth is so closely woven that the cat may suffocate if kept in it long.

Don't try to take a cat on the street in your arms; the swoosh of a truck, a passing dog or any other shock may drive the cat into a panic, and you may get scratched or lose the cat or both.

ON A TRAIN

For train journeys the fiberboard satchels made for cats and dogs are best. They are well ventilated and can't be clawed apart. They look like luggage and consequently are treated with moderate respect by porters. With a thin cushion or a bath mat in the bottom, they are not uncomfortable.

Between journeys the satchel can do duty as a bed for the cat. People who make this double use of carriers seem to find their cats more willing travelers than those who fetch out the satchels at the last moment and pop their cats in.

You must expect the cat to make a fuss at first; no creature likes to be locked in. The worst of it is that they usually quiet down just before the train starts, and then all that noise and vibration and the poor cats yell louder than ever.

Don't put the cat in the baggage car—keep it with you.

Don't feed the cat any soup or vegetables or anything else laxative for at least twenty-four hours before starting on a journey. Give it lean meat and nothing else.

Don't feed the cat at all within four hours of starting time.

Unless you are traveling more than twenty-four hours, don't feed the cat during the journey. It probably won't eat, and if it does the food may not stay put.

Give the cat fresh water every two or three hours—cats get awfully thirsty when they're frightened. Speak to it often and apologize for the inconvenience.

If the journey lasts more than twenty-four hours you'd best take along some cat food. You can't depend on railroads to provide cat meat. Lean boiled beef, lamb, or liver is best. Give the cat about half as much as usual and don't worry if it refuses that.

When traveling with a cat be sure it wears a collar, and that you have a lead handy to snap on the collar every time the satchel is opened. The cat probably won't start home from the middle of nowhere, but this will keep you from worrying.

Don't fuss over the cat, beyond letting it know that you are near and this isn't Judgment Day.

Don't feed the cat the moment you reach your destination. Give it time to sniff around and feel at home.

Cats aren't allowed on busses.

BY CAR

Whatever you do, don't start gallivanting around in a car with a cat at large and unattended. The serenest cat is apt to get playful notions when it sees the world going by at great speed. Playful notions lead to crack-ups.

When Ma, Pickle and Charlie were young and frisky they were taken everywhere in carriers. As they achieved age and dignity they went collared and leashed, with me in the back seat to keep order. Now that Pickle is really old he sits on my lap in the front seat, watches everything and chatters constantly; he is especially fascinated by cows. He is not, even now, allowed to prowl around in a car.

Before starting on a long journey by car I would advise you to read Baron Ireland's delightful poem on taking a cat five hundred miles to Maine—and then take your cat around the corner to the veterinarian and board it there until you come back from the trip. Almost any cat will settle down and make the best of a stay at the vet's, but there are exceptions; Charlie wouldn't eat unless he was with one of us, so we either stayed home or took him with us, and, since it wasn't fair to take Charles and leave Pickle and Ma behind, when we went anywhere it was with three cats.

One trip lasted three weeks and covered more than three thousand miles; to say that the cats were unenthusiastic would be a remarkable understatement. They did not like being dragged out on leashes at every stop. They did not like sleeping in strange beds, even on our feet, though they made a pathetic effort to settle down at each new resting place.

Hotels being adamantly inhospitable to livestock, we stayed at tourist courts, motels, or whatever they're called in your

part of the country, except one night when it was late and raining and we couldn't find such a place, while a hotel was staring us in the eye. Francie thought he might smuggle the cat-
satchel in, but an assiduous bell-boy snatched it and trudged
unsuspectingly ahead, while we held our breath. He opened the
room we were to occupy and set down the luggage. Immediately the cat-satchel began to bulge and wriggle.

The bell-boy stared. "What's in that thing?" he asked.

My husband said, "Snakes," and handed him a dollar.

He disappeared like a magician's rabbit. We waited appre-
hensively for a long time; nothing happened. I don't say this is
an ethical way to get a lodging for the night; on the other
hand, if the cats are quiet and you are equipped with cat pan,
sawdust, food and water dishes for them, I don't see what harm
it can do.

Traveling cats should be fed only once a day, in the evening. It is best to underfeed rather than overfeed them. Canned
cat food is convenient, if you've remembered the can-opener,
and if the cat will eat it—mine won't. Besides, I feel that a cat
away from home and not liking it should have whatever it
fancies for supper, provided the fancy is good for cats.

When visiting friends, relatives, anyone for that matter, it
is advisable to board your cat with a local veterinarian and visit
it every day rather than invade the premises with boodle and
kit. Resident cats are most unlikely to welcome a stranger. If
your host has no cat, the chances are he doesn't want any. (The
only animal we take visiting is our enchanting goat, and then
because Cappy is invited, even urged, to call on friends eager
to rid their property of poison ivy, which Cappy likes better
than good grass.) Frankly, we don't welcome visiting animals
at our house.

DON'T SHIP A CAT

Don't ever ship a cat off alone. Take it with you or leave it behind. My cousin's cat was shipped from Louisville, Kentucky, to Red Bank, New Jersey, a journey that should have been completed within less than twenty-four hours. Little-Little didn't arrive until *FOUR DAYS LATER,* and then the man threw her crate off the train. She weighed eight pounds when she left Louisville; she weighed three pounds when she arrived in Red Bank. And Little-Little had lost her purr; it didn't come back for five months.

Of course most cats that are shipped arrive on time and in good condition, though more frightened than any creature should be. Under the best of conditions it's a cruel experience.

ON MOVING WITH A CAT

The cats used to know when we were going to move almost as soon as we did—we don't move any more, thank heaven. The moment packing commenced they became fretful and restless, pacing, miaouing, crawling into barrels and boxes and almost getting packed. Before the moving men arrived I emptied one room of everything except the cats and their satchels. When the men had gone I put the cats in their carriers and took them to their new home, where they were released in a room the movers wouldn't open, usually a bathroom. There they stayed until all was quiet. When I let them out they would investigate every inch of their new home, sniffing, pawing, feeling with their whiskers, criticizing everything. After they had sat down and washed, I fed them.

HOW TO LEAD A CAT-AND-DOG LIFE

Don't you believe the gingham dog and the calico cat et each other up. They live happily together in millions and millions of homes.

The easiest way to lead a cat-and-dog life is to get a puppy and a kitten and raise them together. They may bark or spit for a day or so and then they'll settle down to be good friends and a lot more fun than either would have been alone.

If you already have a grown dog and you'd like to have a cat, get a kitten. Get a cat if you want to. Cat or kitten, take it first to the vet and have its claws trimmed as close as possible so if it should panic it can't injure the dog's eyes. This is the only time a cat's claws should ever be cut. You'll have to trust the dog to be a gentleman. The safest way to introduce them is to keep both in the house, and separated, for a day or two. That way the cat can smell that a dog lives there, the dog can smell that a cat has arrived, and both will have an opportunity to get used to the idea. The actual introduction should be as casual as possible. If you make a fuss about it you may confuse either or both animals and precipitate a fight that wouldn't otherwise have occurred. Don't show any favoritism and don't scold either animal in the presence of the other. (I used to know a woman who lived with four lion cubs and a fox terrier, and when she scolded the lions the fox terrier barked at her.) Don't go away and leave the dog and cat together until you have seen them eat together and sleep together; from there on they'll be fast friends.

If a cat lives with you and you decide to get a dog the procedure is about the same—the result is anybody's guess. A kitten or a young cat will usually accept a dog in a few days. Old cats, well!

When Pickle was eleven years old and Charlie eight, we got a dog. For us, it was a case of love at first sight and hang the consequences, except the trouble with consequences is that they're with you, hanged or not. Johnny was a German shepherd about five months old (three months older than he should have been). He had the most beautiful head I have ever seen on any dog; also he was wild as a mustang, scared of his shadow, gun-shy, stubborn, and more than usually nearsighted. Certainly not the stuff of which Seeing Eye dogs are made.

Now Pickle and Charlie never had had a dog, nor had they felt the least need of one. To them a dog was an enemy to be routed, and we expected them to tolerate this great galloping lummox! It was unthinkable. Worst of all, Johnny seemed to think they were mere animals, to be mauled if he felt like it, or even chased. He didn't chase cats to harm them, he just liked to make them run. Pickle and Charlie did not choose to run. They never had run from anything, and they didn't aim to start. Being chased did not amuse them.

Just when the situation looked hopeless Charlie accepted the dog. Between them they made up a game; Charlie would roll himself into a tight ball, and Johnny would nudge him all over the house or the lawn. When Charlie had had enough, he would hook a claw in Johnny's neck, pull his head down and hiss in his ear.

Pickle watched these capers with scorn. Months passed before he showed signs of weakening, and then something always happened to break the truce. Johnny would charge into a stone fence after what he blindly took to be a chipmunk, and Pickle would come out raging. Pickle would be watching a mouse-hole, and Johnny would blunder along and spoil the hunting. Pickle would leave a bite on his plate for a bedtime snack, and Johnny would eat it. Always there was Johnny's clatter and fuss; I think the noise, even more than his size, irritated Pickle long after he had discounted Johnny as a menace, for it was only when deafness had muted all sound for Pickle that he made friends with John.

By that time Johnny was downright apprehensive of Pickle, but with immense good will he tried to meet the ornery old cat halfway. Now they're dear friends. Johnny is Pickle's bumbling, fussy, devoted guardian, and Pickle loves it.

X

Accidents and Ailments

Cats are generally healthy, hardy, and enduring creatures, or else they could never have survived centuries of mistreatment. Cats that are well cared for not uncommonly live to be eighteen or nineteen years old, and a considerable number pass twenty.

I once removed a large tumor from a twenty-one-year-old cat and this cat lived to be twenty-three. Cats are highly susceptible, however, to certain diseases such as distemper and can die very quickly if not treated promptly. It is not true that alley cats are hardier and live longer than pet cats. Talk to people from the sanitation department and you will learn how often they find dead cats in the streets, in cellars, and on roads. All we see are the hardiest street cats—those who have survived fights, poor food, bad weather, and numerous other hardships.

Even these hardy ones do not survive for very long unless helped by charitable and generous people who feed and look after them.

In the following pages I have tried to identify most of the things that could happen to a cat, knowing quite well that few of them would happen to any one cat. Besides, most afflictions are under control today if they are treated in time, thanks to the wonderful new medicines that have been developed in the last few years—especially the antibiotics.

Twenty years ago "antibiotic" wasn't even a word in the average person's language. Today penicillin, aureomycin, terramycin, chloramphenicol and the rest of the antibiotics are our main guardians against disease and infection. There is scarcely an infectious condition to which cats are subject that cannot be successfully treated by the use of one or another of the antibiotics. Eye diseases, skin ailments, infected wounds, respiratory afflictions, genitourinary diseases, coccidiosis, even the dreaded enteritis, all respond to one or another of the antibiotics. The methods of administering them are almost as varied as the ailments they can cure. There are injections, pills, capsules, ointments to fit each condition.

Yet remarkable as they are, antibiotics are not the whole story. Antihistamines are of great value in treating respiratory diseases and some skin disorders. There are new medicines for worms that were first developed for the treatment of our troops in the South Pacific during World War II and have now been adapted for use on cats. Hormone therapy keeps old cats (as well as old people) going much longer than anyone would have thought possible a few years ago. Electrocardiographs are used as well as X-rays.

The main thing to remember about the new treatments is

that they they are not home remedies. The penicillin pills you took for that infected tooth are not the thing for Puss. The tablets that relieved your cold were made for people and might kill a cat. Aspirin can badly damage your cat's stomach. Experiments have shown that aspirin can even cause stomach hemorrhage and death. Only a qualified veterinarian knows what to prescribe and in what quantity. Antibiotics and the other new medicines intended for use on cats are obtainable only from the veterinarian or by his prescription. This is to help your cat, not to gouge money out of you.

The information given here about the new treatments is intended as a guide to what the veterinarian can do for your cat. Some veterinarians in communities remote from big-city hospitals may have had little experience with the new reme-dies, or may hesitate to use them unless you ask, and that is one reason for telling you about them. Also, some of the new things are very expensive. Drug companies spend millions of dollars in researching and developing the new drugs, and these costs must ultimately be borne by the consumer. Whether or not the drug companies charge too much for their drugs is a matter for discussion in other types of books. The veterinarian cannot know whether you are able and willing to pay for them unless you tell him. Some people have quaint ideas about the "worth" of an animal. I have heard of people who tearfully had their cat destroyed because they couldn't afford to pay for treatment to save his life and the next day bought a new cat for $100 and more. Each person must decide for himself what his cat is worth to him and the family and act accordingly.

In the following pages I have tried to tell you, as far as possible, how to keep your cat healthy, how to recognize symptoms of serious ailments before they become acute, when to take your cat to the veterinarian and what to expect of him, as well as what you can do on your own or under the doctor's supervision. You can take care of some simple things as well as the veterinarian. You should be able to nurse a sick cat under his supervision and do very well. There are some things you absolutely must not do, and they are possibly the most important of all.

CARDBOARD (ELIZABETHAN) COLLAR

This is a simple item that every cat owner should have on hand at all times. Prompt use of an Elizabethan collar can save your cat and you untold misery. You can often stop a potentially bad condition from developing. For instance, an ear infection may develop into hematoma of the ear flap if the cat scratches the ear. You may save the cat an operation and save yourself a lot of expense and guilt feelings by use of the collar.

As a further example, you may one day see that the membranes around your cat's eyes are redder than usual. This is called conjunctivitis and if treated promptly will generally respond to your veterinarian's care within a reasonable time, depending on its severity. If you cannot get the cat to a veterinarian right away, you should immediately apply an Elizabethan collar. This will prevent the cat from rubbing his eyes with rough hair and dirt on his paws. Rubbing can result in a much more serious condition, such as damage to the eyeball and ulceration of the cornea (outer layer of the eyeball). This condition is much more serious than conjunctivitis and requires more and longer treatment.

To make the collar, get a piece of corrugated cardboard—the type used for cases of canned goods or liquor bottles. A grown

cat weighing about ten pounds will require a piece of cardboard about eleven inches square. The exact size needed for
your cat will vary with his size, strength, and adroitness.

After rounding off the corners of the cardboard to achieve a
rough circle, cut a piece of string to the exact length that fits
closely (but not constrictingly) around your cat's neck. Form
an inner circle with this string in the center of the cardboard
and mark its outline with a pencil; then cut out the marked-off
circle. The round hole in the center of the cardboard will equal
the circumference of the string and thus the size of the cat's
neck.

Now position the cardboard collar by gently pushing it over
the cat's head onto his neck. A battle of wits and patience will
generally ensue. But you must win this battle—with the
knowledge that you are not hurting your cat, that it is really
for the cat's benefit, and that Puss will get used to the collar.

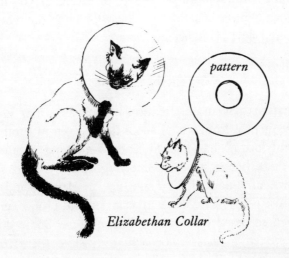

pattern

Elizabethan Collar

Your cat will probably look at you as if you were a torturer and may even yowl for a while. If you do not remove the cardboard collar, he may roll around and tear at it with his feet. Also, he will try to reach the part of his body that itches. He may try to rub his ears or eyes or bite his ear parts. If the collar was properly made he will not be able to reach any of these parts.

If the cat is very strong or works at the collar long enough, he may be able to tear it. You should then make a new one. Puss will be able to sleep and eat very well as the collar bends. Further, most cats get used to the collar and won't bother it after a day or two.

It has been pointed out that the eleven-inch circle is for an average grown cat; experimentation will indicate the exact size needed for your own cat. The collar should be big enough to prevent the cat from hurting himself but not so big that it will prevent him from walking, jumping, or eating. If you have a young kitten, a piece of lighter cardboard, such as the type used for laundered shirts, is sufficient.

VETERINARIANS

Veterinarians pay more attention to cats than they used to and, consequently, know more about them. Even in rural areas "the horse doctor" has had to learn something about cats, partly because horses have become mighty scarce and sheep, goats, cows, and dogs don't make up the deficit—and even more because people who live with cats demand proper care for them. Even so, good cat veterinarians are rare. Some doctors are uninterested in cats; some actually dislike them; others cannot imagine that you are willing to spend good money on a cat, especially a crossbred cat. If you cannot find a veterinarian who is really good at treating cats, make the best of the best one you know; at the worst he knows more about cats than you do. However, in recent years, especially in the larger cities, many veterinarians have developed into cat specialists. They have made a serious study of cats: their diseases, peculiarities, feeding habits, psychology, and so on. If you find one of these, you should do your best to go along with his ideas and not with the advice of your well-meaning friends, relatives, and neighbors.

HOW TO GIVE A CAT A PILL OR CAPSULE

The quickest and easiest way to give a pill or capsule to a cat is as follows:

Put a little butter on the pill or capsule. Then hold the pill between your right thumb and index finger, keeping the butter toward your cat's mouth. Let him lick off some of the butter if he wishes. Now put the cat on a table (scratch-proof top) and pet him with your left hand and talk to him. Keep petting and talking to the cat for a few minutes. Do not hurry. Then use your left hand to press the upper lips of the cat into his upper teeth. This will automatically cause the cat to open his mouth. You then, quickly, use your right thumb and index finger to put the pill as far down the cat's throat as possible.

Do not be afraid to push it down deeply. If you are squeamish and do not put it down deeply enough, the cat will promptly spit out the pill or, worse, crack the pill or capsule and then start frothing. He will not like this and may transfer this dislike to you, and you will have a more difficult time in opening his mouth in the future. Therefore, be bold; put the pill deeply down the cat's throat and you will remain friends, as the pill will go down his throat before he knows what has happened.

If you find that your fingers are awkward in pushing down the pill, do the following: have a long pencil handy with an eraser end and use the same method as described above. As soon as you pop the pill into the back of the throat, use the eraser end of the pencil to push it down further.

If you cannot use the above method, then try to fool the cat. Roll the pill in enough ground lean meat to make a larger pill, not larger than a marble. Make several balls of meat with no pill in them. Give the cat a couple of the pill-less balls as a come-on; then pop in the important one and the cat may never know it. This method almost always works if the pill is small and the cat has not caught you tricking him. However, if he catches you one time, you will probably never be able to do this again.

Large pills, smelly pills, and capsules must be given by force. This does not mean that you must battle the cat for an hour and then give up, with the spitty pill still clutched in your battle-scarred fist. It means you wrap the cat securely in a large towel, a sheet or any other strong cloth—or, best of all, put the cat into an old trouser leg. Having secured the cat, with all claws in, put your left hand over his head, with your thumb over the hinge of the jaw on one side and your middle finger over the jaw hinge on the other side. Gently and firmly press until the cat has to open his mouth. Then quickly put the pill or capsule into the back of the cat's throat, deeply. Shut his mouth and hold it shut, without covering the nostrils, until the cat swallows. Stroking the cat's throat gently downward will make him swallow more quickly. In any case, he has to swallow sometime. If you need to give your cat all or part of a capsule (powder) and have trouble doing it, try this: roll the powder in butter, freeze the ball of powdered butter, then administer like a pill.

HOW TO GIVE A CAT LIQUID MEDICINE

The easiest way, for you, to give a cat liquid medicine is to measure it into a saucer, pretend that it is a good drink, set the saucer on the table, and leave the room. When you come back the saucer may be empty. The success of this method depends upon your cat's nature and the flavor of the medicine. It will work with some cats and not with others. If the cat does not cooperate, you might try this method: Measure the medicine into a saucer; sit down and pretend to drink it; then, when the cat comes around to investigate, share the stuff. This is not often successful, but some cats are deceived by it.

If the above methods do not work, you will then have to force the cat to take the liquid. It is generally best for two people to do this. Measure the dose; then put a little of it into a tablespoon or a plastic medicine dropper—a quarter of a teaspoonful is about all a cat can swallow at one time—and prop the spoon or dropper in a handy place. Spread a towel on a table and stand the cat on the towel. Use the thumb and index finger of your left hand to gently draw out the cheek until a good-sized pocket is formed between the cheek and the teeth in the lower jaw. Take the spoon or dropper in your right hand and slowly dribble the medicine into the pocket. Repeat, a quarter of a teaspoonful at a time, until the whole dose is in the cat.

Never allow the cat to raise his head much above the horizontal level, for if you do the liquid may go down his windpipe into the lungs and cause mechanical pneumonia, which could kill him. If the cat fights, wrap him up so that he cannot scratch, or get someone to hold his front feet; but whatever you do, be sure the cat does not tip his head back and choke.

This is the only safe way to give a cat liquid medicine against his will. If the cat spits it out, start over again. Keep petting and talking to your cat at all times so that he will be reassured. Try to hold his head as still as possible, so that he will not spray the liquid all over you and the room.

HOW TO FEED A CAT LIQUID FOOD

Sometimes it is necessary to feed a sick cat liquid food. The mixture that has worked best for me is strained baby food (the meat type) with enough warm water added to make a soup. You can try any type of meat to tempt your cat, but it is generally best to use the meat that the cat preferred before he got sick—chicken, liver, lamb, kidney, beef, veal, or whatever.

It has been my experience that the cat will generally, after a few days of forced feeding, come to the conclusion that you do not intend to let him starve under any circumstances. Therefore, he decides that he'd better start eating by himself and thus end the bother of being force-fed. For this reason, always keep some of the baby food without the added water in a dish on the floor where the cat can get at it. The cat will eventually start eating this food by himself. You can then gradually get him back on his regular diet. You can also scrape some fresh raw meat and make a small ball out of it and pop it down the cat's throat just like a pill.

When force-feeding the cat with soupy baby food, you might

try to put it into a baby's nursing bottle, with the hole in the nipple slightly enlarged; cuddle the cat until he is fairly comfortable; and slide the nipple into his mouth. If the cat will not take it this way, force-feed with a spoon or plastic medicine dropper as described under HOW TO GIVE A CAT LIQUID MEDICINE.

EXTERNAL PARASITES

External parasites often cause allergies in cats to a lesser or greater degree. Some cats are very sensitive, others less sensitive, and some are practically insensitive, so that the parasites will not cause any itchiness at all. It is often necessary to treat a bitten cat with anti-allergy medicine to stop the itching sensation, even after all the parasites have been killed, in order to eliminate the allergy.

FLEAS

Fleas ruin the cat's coat, spread tapeworm, carry disease, and make the cat miserable all over. Experienced cat fleas prefer cats, but youthful fleas have a tendency to jump around and try anything once—even you if you are not careful.

Some tapeworm larvae hitchhike on fleas. Cats can get dog tapeworm from biting fleas that have been associating with dogs.

Cat Flea  *actual size ⅛ inch*

Adult fleas live and love and lay their eggs right on the cat. The eggs drop off and develop into maggoty little worms, which in turn spin cocoons about the size of grains of wheat around themselves and settle down in dark and dusty corners to meditate and grow. In a couple of weeks they come out looking for a cat.

It is possible to get fleas off a cat. It is impossible to keep them off as long as there are dusty corners. Fleas love damp basements, garages, the ground under the porch, and any old corner where dust lies undisturbed. Pyrethrum preparations or cabaryl scattered in flea corners will kill the larvae effectively. Soap, water, elbow grease, and pyrethrum preparations will help keep fleas out of the house.

The right kind of flea spray or powder will keep cats free of fleas. The wrong kind will make cats sick, irritate their skin, or even kill them.

Most of the flea powders recommended for use on dogs are unsafe for cats. Some that are specially packaged for cats are unsafe if the cat licks them. Never buy flea powder without reading the label carefully: Even the good kind you used last summer may have been "improved" by a pinch of this or a dab of that to make it different—and the cat sick.

Flea powder that is safe to use on cats contains pyrethrum, cabaryl, derris and rotenone, which is the resin of derris, and inert matter such as talcum or cornstarch—and *nothing else*.

The list of ingredients on the label should look something like this:

Rotenone 1.00%   Other cube resins 1.00%   Pyrethrins 0.05%
Inert ingredients 97.95%

or

Cabaryl 3.00%   2.2 Methylenebis 0.50%
Inert ingredients 96.50%

If any other ingredients *of any nature whatsoever* are listed, don't buy that brand of flea powder for a cat.

The effectiveness of flea powder depends considerably upon the method of application. First, you sprinkle a good dab of powder on the back of the cat's neck. Then work it through his fur down to the skin and all the way around the cat's neck, up over his head and down around the cheeks and chin. Put a pinch of powder in front of each ear and work the powder into the fur in the outer ear, but not down inside the ear. Protect the cat's eyes, and be careful also not to get powder into his nose. Powder the rear just as thoroughly, and rub some between the toes of each foot. Powder the back and the underside, making sure to cover the belly area especially well, as that is where the fleas love to congregate. Then give a final dash of powder under the tail.

If the cat doesn't lick the powder off, that is all you need do. Some cats, however, cannot rest until they have licked off all the powder and made themselves ill. If your cat is a powder licker, wrap him in a cloth and hold it on for at least fifteen minutes, to give the chemicals a chance to work. Then brush the powder out as thoroughly as you worked it in, brushing against the fur as well as with it. Licking powder of a suitable formula won't do the cat any real harm, since derris and rotenone in flea-powder doses are not toxic to cats, but there's no point in having your pet a little ill.

A few cats are allergic to any sort of powder, and about the only thing to do for them is comb out the fleas painstakingly, one by one. It would be helpful to use a flea comb. This is a special comb, made of metal, which has very fine teeth placed close together. While combing the cat, keep him on a newspaper, and burn or otherwise effectively dispose of the paper at once.

Another helpful device is a cat flea collar. Before using such a collar, which works by emitting a special chemical gas, you should always expose the collar to air for three hours after removing it from the package it is wrapped in. This will allow the excess chemical gas to evaporate before the collar is put on the cat.

A cat that lives in an apartment and does not go out will not have fleas unless he has preserved a few from his past, or unless somebody or something brings them in. Fleas do not just happen.

SOME DON'TS

Never, never use anything containing creosote, tar, naphthalene, phenol (carbolic acid), or creolin on or near a cat. They are deadly.

No preparation containing DDT can be used on or near or even in the same quarters with cats. DDT, chlordane, and the other modern vermin killers are all harmful to cats. It isn't even safe to use them on lawns or gardens where cats play, because if cats walk on poisoned grass or brush against shrubbery coated with it, and lick themselves, they may die. These things are wonderful in their place. Their place is not on cats.

STICKTIGHT FLEAS

The sticktight is a true Southerner, it cannot stand a cold climate. It is small, black, and glossy. You do not catch a sticktight hopping around on a hot day the way Yankee fleas do. You don't catch a sticktight climbing around in a lot of fur, either. He finds a nice juicy bare spot, settles down, and eats his fill. He is not choosy—cats, dogs, people, chickens, rats, anything with warm red blood is fine.

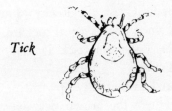

Tick

actual size of male ⅛ inch
female ¼ to ⅜ inch

Epicurean sticktights prefer cats' ears, the rims of which are thinly furred and pink and sensitive. Sticktights settle shoulder to shoulder and nose to tail in a mourning band all around the cat's ears, and then you try to get them off. Just try! Flea powder will not stick to the rims of cats' ears, and neither will anything else, except sticktights. Besides flea powder, try hand picking, flea spray (cat brands only), and a flea collar. You might also try some Vicks VapoRub or Boroleum on the cat's ears.

LICE

Lice are nasty little grayish or brownish things that crawl slowly around on cats and ruin their coats. You can easily distinguish them from the lively northern flea. Lice also deposit tiny pearl-like larvae (nits) on the cat's hairs. Treat lice the same way as fleas, but check the skin and coat every few days. If any lice are still in evidence, repeat the treatment.

TICKS

Ticks are bugs that suck the blood of man or beast. The ticks that get on cats are called dog ticks because they prefer dogs, but they will settle for cats.

Cats that go outdoors east of the Rocky Mountains must

beware of the American dog tick, alias the eastern wood tick. From the Rockies to the Pacific Coast, the Rocky Mountain spotted fever tick, or western wood tick, is a real menace, since it spreads spotted fever. The Lone Star tick is said to be working its way north from Texas.

Even cats that lead cloistered lives in city apartments must beware of ticks, for that is where the brown tick lives. The brown tick is an alien that entered the country some years ago and is already a pest, particularly in homes where there are dogs. Since the brown tick lives only in houses, or very close to them, it could be eradicated if people would call in a competent exterminator at the first sign of one. The brown tick sets up housekeeping in any warm crack or crevice—behind walls, in a corner of the fireplace, in books, in paintings, and in many other spots. So getting rid of him is no job for an amateur.

Ticks attach themselves to cats, or any other creatures they fancy, by chewing through the skin and burrowing part way in. The body, which stays outside, becomes a big brown blob as it fills with blood. As an extra-gruesome touch, the tick carries its own anesthetic, so the victim doesn't even know its blood is being sucked.

Ticks should be removed by hand. But do not pull them out by brute force; violence may wrench off only the body and leave part of the tick to fester embedded in the cat. Do not remove ticks with your bare hands, for there is a slight chance of contracting Rocky Mountain spotted fever, which is very bad indeed and much more bother than putting on rubber gloves.

To remove ticks by hand you need a pair of tweezers; a little alcohol, ether, or chloroform to anesthetize the ticks; and enough alcohol to kill the bugs after they have been removed.

You put a drop of your chosen anesthetic on the tick, wait a minute until it is unconscious, and then lift it off with the tweezers. Always grasp the tick at its head, as close to the cat's skin as possible, so that no part of the tick will be left on the skin. Ticks are very tough insects and it may be necessary to crush them in order to kill them. Ordinarily, ticks are not very important problems in households where only cats and no dogs exist. However, you may sometimes find ticks on your cat every day even though you keep taking them off. In such a case you can be pretty sure that your house is infested with ticks and it would be best to call an experienced tick exterminator.

SKIN DISEASES

INTRODUCTION

Cats develop many different types of skin diseases. To the untrained eye some of the diseases may look very similar. For this reason, they are often mistreated in accordance with some neighbor's advice. The following paragraphs contain descriptions of the principal skin diseases in order to show their range. If Puss develops skin trouble, however, I would urge you to take him, promptly, to a veterinarian for proper diagnosis and treatment. Otherwise a simple condition might develop into a long-drawn-out difficult ailment.

REDDENING

Acute Dermatitis

Symptoms: Red areas on skin. May or may not be itchy.

Causes: Allergy, parasite bites, injury, burns, excess sun, others.

Chronic Dermatitis

Symptoms: Thickening and often darkening of skin.

Causes: Same as those of acute dermatitis (see above).

Nettle Rash
(Hives—Urticaria)

Symptoms: Swelling of skin, lips, eyelids, etc.; development of wheals.

Causes: Cat's special sensitivity to something he ate, inhaled, or touched. A cat may suddenly develop an allergy to something that has not bothered him previously even though he has had contact with it for many years. For example, a ten-year-old cat may suddenly develop skin symptoms after eating cooked liver though it may never have bothered him before.

BALDNESS

Symptoms: Loss of hair.

Causes: Change of diet, previous illness, climatic changes, poor diet, hormone abnormality, infections, parasites, drugs, burns, chemicals, tumors.

DANDRUFF

Symptoms: Flakes of dead skin on the hair or the skin.

Causes: Dry skin, climatic changes, dietary deficiency, hormone abnormality, mite infestation.

MITE INFESTATION
(Cheyletiella)

Symptoms: Scaling, later crusting of the skin. Cat may or may not itch.

Cause: Mites.

Mange Mite  *visible under magnification*

EAR-MITE MANGE

(Notoedric Mange)

Symptoms: Very itchy, crusty inflammation of skin, leading to baldness. Mostly seen on head of cat in and around ears.

Cause: Mite which can be seen only under magnification. See paragraph under EAR DISEASES describing ear mites and their treatment.

HORMONE DISTURBANCES

Symptoms: Vary with the specific hormone that is causing the condition. In general, hormone dysfunction will cause baldness, dullness of the coat, scaling, and sometimes blackness of the skin. Also, the cat may itch.

Cause: Abnormality of the thyroid, adrenal, or pituitary glands or the testicles or ovaries.

BACTERIAL INFECTION

Symptoms: Small pus-filled eruptions on the skin.

Causes: Bacteria, generally staphylococci.

FURUNCULOSIS

Symptoms: A widespread bacterial infection of the skin that infects the hair follicles very deeply. This disease will often deeply destroy tissues of the feet and lips and may cause ulcers to develop.

Cause: Virulent bacteria.

ULCERS

Symptoms: Destruction of skin which extends deep enough to form a shallow hole in the skin.

Cause: Generally bacterial.

FUNGUS

Symptoms: Different fungi produce different lesions on the cat's skin. In one form, you will see a round lesion with a reddish border. You may see only dry-looking skin or scabby patches. You may see reddish, yellowish, or grayish patches of skin, especially on the face or between the toes. The skin may feel gritty.

Causes: Various fungi.

Practically all fungus infections of the cat are transmissible to people. Therefore, you should pay particular attention to this condition and have your cat treated promptly if you see any suspicious lesions.

MANGE

Mange is caused by microscopic mites. Cats are not nearly as subject to mange as dogs are, but they can catch and spread it. There are two kinds of mange: sarcoptic and follicular. Sarcoptic looks worse: follicular is worse.

In the early stages, sarcoptic and follicular mange resemble each other and both resemble ringworm, eczema, and the skin rashes caused by internal worms; so don't try to be the cat's diagnostician. Only a well-informed veterinarian with a microscope can tell you which skin ailment your cat has and how to cure it.

To make a diagnosis, he will scrape a little skin off a bare spot and examine it under the microscope. The doctor may have to make several scrapings before he can be sure.

Mange usually starts around the eyes, at the base of the ears, or under the forelegs near the body. It rarely begins in a place the cat can reach with his tongue when he washes.

Sarcoptic mange begins as little blisters that break and separate and form scabs. The hair falls out. The scabs become scaly. The cat scratches himself, and soon there are nasty sores all over the body.

Follicular mange is insidious. At first it shows as small, scaly patches, grayish or merely bare and not very itchy. The patches spread fast and soon the skin becomes grayish or brick-dust-colored and wrinkled like the skin of an old elephant. The hair falls out. The cat becomes emaciated and dull. Follicular mange has a toxic effect on the cat which devitalizes him. If neglected, it may kill him.

The treatment and cure of mange used to be one of the most long-drawn-out and miserable chores a person could take on. In the case of follicular mange, veterinarians often advised having the animals killed, because people just wouldn't stick with the treatment until the cure was complete. Curing follicular mange is now much easier to do, but still requires the attention of a veterinarian.

Don't expect every veterinarian to hospitalize an animal with mange. Unless he has an isolation ward, one mangy cat might infect his whole hospital. Treatment is a job you often have to do yourself.

The chance of a human being's getting mange from a cat is

very remote, since we are not very hairy and we bathe often. If it should happen, the ailment can be treated successfully.

TUMORS

Symptoms: More or less hard swellings on or below the skin. *Causes:* Mostly unknown. Some tumors are said to be caused by irritation, viruses, damage to the skin.

EAR DISEASES

EAR MITES

Ear mites are similar to sarcoptic mange mites, except that they specialize in ears and the skin around the ears. Ear mites generally require magnification to be clearly seen.

Mange Mite   *visible under magnification*

A cat with ear mites shakes his head and paws at his ears or rubs them against trees, furniture, or anything handy. Deep inside his ears you can see, with an otoscope, caked black greasy stuff. Sometimes the whole ear is inflamed from mites and scratching. I have never heard of a person's catching ear mites from a cat.

The cure should be left to the veterinarian, because cats' ears are delicate and amateur probing can do a great deal of harm. If you are willing to risk injuring the cat's ears in order to try to cure it yourself, this is the safest way: use a Q-Tip moistened with heavy mineral oil. Wipe one ear tenderly and thoroughly, following and cleaning each convolution. When the ears are thoroughly cleaned, apply a little plain boric acid powder into the ear. Repeat the same procedure with the other ear. Do this two or three times a week, until the swabs do not pick up any more dirt when inserted in the ear canals. Since the Q-Tips, after use in the ears, will contain live ear mites, it is best to dispose of them by flushing down the toilet.

NONPARASITIC EAR DISEASES

Symptoms: Same as those of ear mites.
Causes: Injuries, inflammation, general weakness, dirt.
Treatment: The cat should be examined and treated by a veterinarian.

SWELLINGS

ABSCESSES

Abscesses may be caused by scratches or bites from other cats or, more commonly, by rat bites. They are very dangerous to cats and if not properly treated may recur again and again until the cat gives up and dies. The first abscess appears at the place of infection, and others may follow in a sort of chain. Abscesses caused by rat or cat bites usually appear on the face or shoulders. They are sometimes as large as hen's eggs.

Any sudden lump or swelling on a cat should be regarded as a serious ailment and the cat should be taken to the vet at once. Surgery of one type or another may be required. Abscesses are dangerous and extremely painful and must have skilled attention.

The antibiotics are of enormous value here. Cats that would have suffered long misery, or even died, can be made well very quickly through injections of penicillin or other antibiotics plus an operation on the abscess if necessary. If your cat is bitten by another cat or other animal, it would be best to have your veterinarian examine your cat since an abscess may form under the skin and not show any skin swelling.

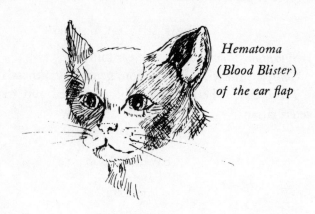

Hematoma (Blood Blister) of the ear flap

BLOOD CYSTS

(Hematoma)

Blood cysts are caused by severe bruises that fail to lacerate the skin but break a blood vessel under it. Most hematomas result from the cat's rubbing or scratching with his paw at an ear flap, usually in an effort to gain relief from irritation caused by infestation with mites. Blood cysts may also be caused by cat bites, dog bites, slamming of a door on the cat's tail, or other injuries. The blood cyst consists of a globule of blood under the skin—sometimes quite large, always painful. It generally requires surgery.

INTERNAL PARASITES

INTRODUCTION

Kittens do not always have worms. If the Queen (mother cat) is free of worms and the kittens are kept under sanitary conditions, the kittens probably won't have worms. Worms come only from other worms, not from candy, dirt, raw meat (if it contains no worms), or similar matter. However, cats can get trichinosis from raw or undercooked pork and some worms from certain raw fish.

Worms do not go away in time; on the contrary, they may outlast the kitten. However, "a good dose of worm medicine" is not a cure-all, even when the cat has worms; there are worms and worms, and one worm's poison may be another worm's meat. Haphazard dosing with worm medicine probably kills more kittens than worms kill.

The patent medicines sold as vermifuges vary a great deal. Even the best of them, those which contain ingredients the veterinarian would prescribe, should be used only if he does prescribe them and advises you to worm the cat at home. The best and safest of the commercial vermifuges may be put up in doses too strong for your cat.

Never, never give a kitten or a cat any vermifuge intended for puppies or dogs.

Never give a cat castor oil unless the doctor tells you to. Castor oil is not a home remedy for cats. Even a small dose may be dangerously strong.

Symptoms of worm infestation: Although several kinds of worms infest cats, their effect is about the same, because they steal the cats' food and weaken them. A wormy cat is usually thin and potbellied; his coat is dry and poor and sheds a lot.

His breath usually has a peculiar sickening-sweet odor. The cat
is both listless and nervous. He may lose his appetite or may
become ravenous; in either case, his attitude toward food is out
of the ordinary. Kittens severely infested with stomach worms
may vomit them or pass them in the bowel movement. Some
cats have large or small infestations of worms and show practically no symptoms.

If the kitten, or cat, is seriously infested with worms, it is best
to have the veterinarian do the worming. If you are not near a
veterinarian and must worm the cat yourself, get worm medicine (made for cats only) for the particular worm that your cat
has. Then follow directions exactly. It is always best to give
warm-water enemas several hours after the medicine has been
given even if the directions on a worm-medicine box do not
mention this. (For discussion of enemas, see CONSTIPATION.)

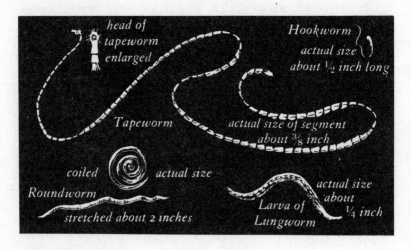

Internal Parasites

ROUNDWORMS

Cause: The adult worm ranges from 1½ to 7 inches long and may be coughed up, vomited, or passed in the stool.

Symptoms: Potbelly, cough, hiccups, pneumonia, poor condition, diarrhea, vomiting, skin trouble.

Life cycle: Worm eggs either are ingested by the cat or enter the blood stream of a kitten while it is still in the uterus of an infested mother. The eggs develop in the intestine of the cat into larvae, which then enter the blood and lymph circulation and end up in the lungs. Here they develop into adult worms, which are then coughed up. If the cat instead of spitting out the worms then swallows them, they move out through the bowel movement. While in the intestine of the cat the adult worm lays its eggs, and the whole cycle starts over. Soon the eggs also pass out in the bowel movement along with the adult worms. Another cat may come along, step on these eggs, get them on his paws, and lick his paws to clean himself, and in this way another cat becomes infested and the cycle starts again in the new cat.

HOOKWORMS

Cause: A hookworm is a small, thin worm ranging from ⅜ to ¾ inch long.

Symptoms: Diarrhea, often very dark stool, rough coat, poor condition, cough, anemia. One adult hookworm, in twenty-four hours, can remove as much as 0.1 cc of blood. From this we can see what a tremendous amount of blood a cat can lose if heavily infested with hookworms.

Life cycle: A cat may swallow the worm eggs, larvae may penetrate the skin, or the kitten may be infested while still in the uterus of the mother. The larvae cannot survive freezing temperatures.

Cause: A tapeworm is a long worm, sometimes consisting of hundreds of segments (proglottids), which contain its eggs. You may see the segments as white, pink, or brownish-looking particles in the cat's bowel movement. Each segment is about the size of a grain of rice. The segments dry, shrivel and turn brown when exposed to air.

Life cycle: Cats generally get tapeworms by swallowing fleas, lice, rodents, or fish that contain tapeworm eggs.

Prevention: It is important that the cat not come into contact with fleas, lice, or rodents. When the cat is wormed, you may see many tapeworm segments in the stool. However, it is essential that the head of the tapeworm be eliminated—otherwise it will grow new segments.

(Aelurostrongylus)

Symptoms: Chronic respiratory trouble with coughing and difficult breathing. This is a very uncommon condition in the United States.

(Strongyloides)

Cause: The threadworm is a thin worm. The larva, which comes out in the feces, resembles the larva of the lungworm.

Symptoms: May cause bronchial pneumonia in kittens, diarrhea (may be bloody), poor condition, eye trouble. Adult cats sometimes have no symptoms at all.

Life cycle: Cat swallows larvae, or larvae may penetrate skin.

HEARTWORMS

Cause: The heartworm is of various sizes, generally about 1½ inches long. It usually inhabits the right side of the heart.

Symptoms: Coughing and difficult breathing, sometimes spitting up of blood, dullness, weakness, and heart trouble.

Life cycle: Cat swallows a mosquito that contains heartworm larvae. The larvae remain in the tissues of the cat for three to four months, then migrate through the veins of the cat to the heart. They then develop into adult worms in the cat's heart.

COCCIDIOSIS

Cause: Small parasite which can be seen only under magnification.

Symptoms: This condition mostly affects young cats and may cause chronic diarrhea with bleeding.

Life cycle: In its oöcyst state, this parasite lives in the ground. When the cat eats an oöcyst, it sporulates in the cat's intestine into different forms of parasites, which enter the epithelial cells lining the intestine. After more development they leave the cells and are expelled with the bowel movement. Therefore, cleanliness and sanitation are very important in preventing infestation.

TOXOPLASMOSIS

This is a disease, mostly of young cats, that may occur in various forms—bronchial pneumonia, pancreas and liver infection, inflammation of the heart muscle, and others. The eyes often become cloudy, and fever persists no matter what the cat is given. It is very difficult to cure this affliction. Further, it is transmissible to people. Therefore, a cat with any of the above

symptoms should have a veterinarian's care as soon as possible.
This disease is caused by a protozoan parasite.

STOMACH TROUBLES

VOLUNTARY REVERSE GEAR

The reverse gear of a cat's digestive system is swift and
usually wonderful. Whatever the cat's stomach doesn't like, the
cat throws up. A cat can regurgitate its dinner, merely because
it doesn't sit right in the stomach, without being the least bit
ill.

When cats are very hungry they sometimes vomit froth and
a little yellowish fluid. If you feed the cat before he gets too
hungry, you won't have that to clean up.

There are times, not often, when Puss eats the wrong thing
and does not vomit quickly. This can lead to trouble and
require treatment.

INVOLUNTARY REVERSE GEAR

When a cat is sick he vomits miserably, retching and gag-
ging. This may be due to hair balls, too much grass or other
vegetable matter in the stomach, worms, constipation, poisoning, enteritis, or any one of a dozen other troubles.

You can make a possible diagnosis by examining the vomit.
A wad of hair or grass blades or anything of the sort calls for a
good dose of whatever you are accustomed to giving the cat for
hair balls, and no food that day. The presence of worms calls
for a trip to the veterinarian.

Repeated vomiting, blood streaks, brown or greenish color,
or any peculiar odor should send you scurrying to the veterinarian with the cat.

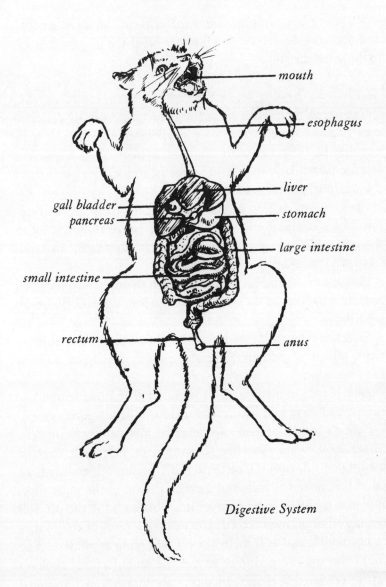

mouth

esophagus

liver

gall bladder

stomach

pancreas

large intestine

small intestine

rectum

anus

Digestive System

Vomiting is merely the outward evidence of inner trouble, and you and the cat are much better off if the diagnosis is left to the veterinarian.

HAIRBALLS

Cats clean themselves by licking their fur, and in doing so they swallow loose hair. If they swallow enough hair, it mats together in their stomachs and forms hairballs. Long-haired cats are particularly subject to hairballs, and all cats get them if they are not brushed regularly.

Country cats, whose people do not brush them, do it themselves by scratching off loose hair on bushes or rolling it off in the grass. Also, the grass they nibble helps to prevent hairballs from staying in them.

House cats depend on people to brush them. If the people do not, the cats have to do all their own grooming, and the result is hairballs.

Sometimes hairballs work down and form intestinal obstructions, which are serious. Others are vomited as hard wads or felt-like strips.

Any bland, unmedicated oil or fat will remove hairballs— except, as I have said before, that castor oil is much too violent for a cat's insides and should never be given indiscriminately. Mineral oil, white Vaseline, Laxatone, or Petromalt may be used. Olive oil, corn oil, cottonseed oil, peanut oil, and soybean oil will remove hairballs and nourish the cat at the same time. Butter is useful as a preventive; it is also useful if the cat will not lap oil of his own accord: you can put a piece of cold butter in his mouth, and as it melts the cat will often swallow it. You could also use margarine or any of the manufactured cooking fats or rendered beef suet. In short, any unmedicated, unsalted fat or oil that you yourself would use is a safe hairball remover. Never give a cat harsher laxatives for hairballs.

The dose varies with the size and age of the cat. A teaspoonful for a kitten, two teaspoonfuls for a half-grown cat, or a tablespoonful for a big cat should remove hairballs within a few hours. If the first dose doesn't work, give another the next day. If the cat has a lot of hairballs, three doses may be necessary. Pure, edible fat or oil cannot possibly harm the cat.

Most cats will lap oil or fat from a saucer, especially the oil from a can of sardines. Or you can smear it on the cat's paws or around his lips to cause him to lick it off. If this does not succeed, you will have to administer a dose.

Once the hairballs are out of the cat, keep them out. A good system of prevention is to brush Puss daily, twice a day if possible, and give about one-fourth to one-half teaspoon daily of Laxatone, Petromalt, or Femalt.

CONSTIPATION

Constipation may be caused by hairballs, some other intestinal obstruction, improper feeding, or, rarely, lack of exercise. A sick cat that has a fever may become constipated because of the dehydrating effect of the fever. Old cats very often become constipated because their bowel action slows down.

People often think a cat is constipated when he actually has urinary obstruction. The cat squats often and strains and does not do anything, so the diagnosis is not illogical; it is just terribly, terribly wrong. Having made the diagnosis, what could be more natural than to give the cat a laxative? That is even worse: the very last thing a cat with kidney stones or gravel should have is a laxative. That cat needs a doctor, and quick.

Hairballs and unsuitable diet are the commonest causes of constipation and the easiest to cope with. A dose of salad oil or a meal of raw liver should change the situation, and some modification of the diet ought to keep it corrected.

If the cat is severely constipated, an adult-size glycerine suppository should be inserted in the rectum (the body opening just below the base of the tail). You should always have a jar of adult-size glycerine suppositories in the refrigerator. These suppositories may look very big, but you will find them easy to administer if proper directions are followed.

Apply a liberal amount of white Vaseline on the tip of the suppository. Then lift the cat's tail with one hand and quickly push the suppository (Vaseline end first) into the rectum as deeply as you can. Now, with the tail down, hold the base of the tail against the rectum so that the cat cannot eject the suppository before it has a chance to melt. This melted glycerine suppository will cause the cat to move his bowels.

It may take two or three suppositories to produce satisfactory results; the number depends on the degree of constipation and the ingenuity and stubbornness of your particular cat. Sometimes these are not sufficient and you may need to use a laxative suppository such as Dulcolax or Senokot. These are used in the same way as the glycerine suppositories.

If laxative or glycerine suppositories do not correct the constipation, you can try an enema. Add a little Ivory soap to lukewarm (not hot) water. Then fill a one-ounce all-rubber ear syringe with the warm soapy solution. Make sure there is no air in the syringe. To do this, hold up the tip of the syringe and squeeze it till a little soap solution comes out; then fill the bulb again and repeat the process till there is no air left in the syringe. Then apply a liberal amount of white Vaseline on the tip of the syringe.

The next step is to hold the cat's tail up with one hand, insert the tip of the syringe into the rectum, and squeeze the bulb of the syringe. Keep squeezing the bulb until all the water is in the cat's rectum. It is best to hold the syringe in the rectum for a few minutes so that the cat cannot eject the soapy solution too quickly.

The ease with which you will give the enema depends, largely, on your cat's disposition. I would recommend that you seek the aid of one, preferably two persons, to hold the front and middle parts of the cat, using heavy towels or blankets. Instead of the ear syringe, you may use a Fleet's enema, which is pre-prepared.

It may be that the cat's trouble is not a simple constipation, in which the stool is in the rectum. Sometimes the unabsorbed material is deeper in the bowels, much nearer the stomach, and the cat keeps straining to get it out. This results in the ejection from the rectum of the watery part of the matter while the hard matter remains and builds up into a rock-like mass. It would be very dangerous to give a laxative (the intestine might rupture), and ordinarily enemas and suppositories do not help this condition at all. This is definitely a case for a veterinarian.

The following are safe laxatives for cats: olive oil, mineral oil, white Vaseline, butter, beef suet, Petromalt, Femalt, Laxatone, margarine, any of the manufactured cooking fats and milk of magnesia (half a teaspoonful or one tablet is the usual dose).

You must never give a cat any commercial laxative prepared for humans—not even if it is "safe enough to give a baby." A number of commercial laxatives for human use contain small amounts of strychnine, just enough to make people feel better —enough sometimes to kill a cat.

Veterinarians often prescribe Vitamin B complex for old cats whose digestive processes have slowed down.

Let me repeat that in many cats, it would be best to give about one-fourth to one-half teaspoonful of Laxatone, Petromalt, or Femalt daily and try to prevent both hairballs and constipation.

SIMPLE DIARRHEA

Diarrhea may be caused by any sudden change of diet: from cooked liver to raw, cooked beef to canned food, lean meat to fat. Cats that have been undernourished and suddenly find themselves well fed may have diarrhea, at least for a time, simply because they aren't accustomed to good food.

Kaopectate, Kalpec, or Pectocel, all of which can be bought at the drugstore, should check simple diarrhea due to change of food within a day. Give one teaspoonful every four hours until the cat is normal.

If, despite treatment, the diarrhea continues into the second day, it is no longer simple, and the cat should be taken to the veterinarian.

FOREIGN BODIES

Cats lack the avidity of dogs in collecting indigestible curiosa, but they do pick up needles and pins, chicken bones, fish bones, and a few other odds and ends, including great lengths of string.

A cat with an obstruction in his throat gags and coughs and paws at his mouth. Before he has a chance to swallow what he should not, or becomes frantic and injures himself, drop a coat or a blanket over him to prevent thrashing and scratching. Then, with a finger on each side of his cheeks, press the lips in until the cat opens his mouth wide. Look down his throat, with a flashlight if possible. If a knobby bone is stuck in the throat, you can probe with two fingers and very likely take it out.

If you see a sharp bone or any other sharp object, get the cat to the veterinarian with as little fuss and delay as possible. *Do not* try to take fish bones, chicken bones, needles, or pins out of a cat's throat unless it is plain that you can work them out without doing any damage. To remove such objects properly, the veterinarian must usually administer a general anesthetic.

If you do not see anything in the cat's throat, turn him loose for a few minutes and watch. If he continues to fret or show any sign of discomfort, hurry him to the veterinarian.

If the cat seems unconcerned after your inspection of his throat, he may nevertheless have swallowed something troublesome in trying to get it out. There is no harm in assuming that he did. Corrective measures must be taken right away, not a few hours later or the next day.

If you cannot possibly get the cat to a veterinarian, try the following:

First, feed the cat all he will eat of anything bulky and soft: potatoes, bread soaked in broth, boiled boned fish, rice with gravy, or anything of the sort. When the cat won't eat another bite, put half a teaspoonful of salt in the back of his mouth to bring the food up again. This may or may not bring up the indigestible oddity. If it does, and you think that is all of it, apologize to the cat and keep an eye on him for a day or so. If nothing unusual appears, watch him closely for any swelling of the abdomen, vomiting, or diarrhea. In case of any of these symptoms, the veterinarian will have to X-ray your cat.

Kittens often swallow string—sometimes yards and yards of string. The best treatment, provided no needle is attached, is the same as for hairballs.

Sometimes a kitten swallows part of a string and leaves the rest hanging out of his mouth. It is not safe to try to pull the string out. Just cut it off as close as you can, give the kitten enough salad oil to grease the string thoroughly, and watch for the other end. If two or three doses of oil don't fetch the string, you had better have the veterinarian remove it.

Most cats that swallow strange things do so by accident. A few have perverse appetites and chew up blankets, bath towels, straw hats—even the litter in their pans—on purpose.

ANAL-GLAND INFECTION

Cats sometimes get an infection of the anal glands, located just inside the anus. When infected, they swell up and cause discomfort. You should have your veterinarian take care of this.

CONTAGIOUS DISEASES

FELINE ENTERITIS

(Distemper, Cat Plague, Panleukopenia)

This is a powerful, highly contagious virus disease. The virus is so strong that a cat may get sick and die within eight hours. It is therefore essential that you take your cat to a veterinarian as soon as you recognize one or more of the possible symptoms. Kittens are the most frequent, and easiest, victims. One presumptive symptom is that the kitten will hover over a dish of water and look very thirsty but won't drink. He will then develop dullness, stop playing, stop eating and drinking: he may vomit yellow material and may become feverish.

So contagious is this disease that it sometimes kills every affected kitten in an area and a large percentage of adult cats.

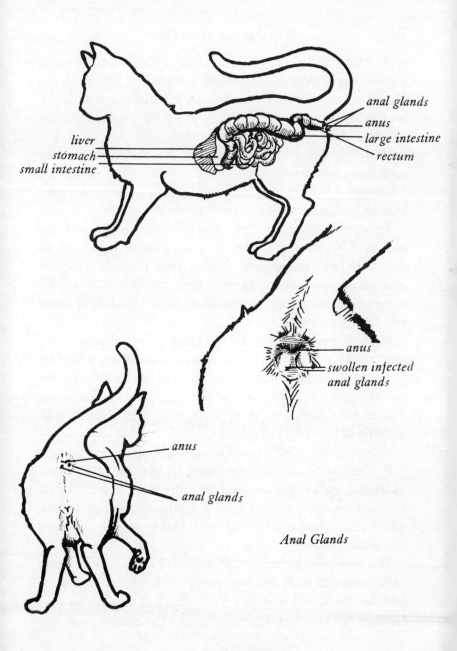

anal glands
anus
large intestine
rectum

liver
stomach
small intestine

anus
swollen infected
anal glands

anus

anal glands

Anal Glands

Outbreaks usually occur in the spring or fall. After doing its terrible work, enteritis may vanish for a while, then reappear. Cats that have survived enteritis seem to be immune, and their owners sort of forget the whole thing—until another epidemic strikes. I advise you not to forget it.

Most cases of feline enteritis can be prevented, or their severity can be lessened, by vaccination. For this purpose, a serum and a vaccine have been developed. The serum has been very helpful in protecting kittens against enteritis until they are old enough for the vaccine, which confers permanent immunity. Though the vaccination is not absolutely perfect, cats that have been immunized usually come through epidemics without so much as a sneeze. Many, many cats that have already contracted the disease have been saved by prompt veterinary treatment.

Enteritis may be transmitted by infected cats, fleas, and any article with which sick cats have come into contact, including people's hands, their clothing, and the soles of their shoes. Also, the virus may be airborne. Therefore, your cat may get distemper even though he never leaves your home; that is why you should have him vaccinated.

A cat with enteritis can hold his own as long as he is stronger than the disease and keeps wanting to live. He is far more likely to keep wanting to live if he is nursed at home. The cat must receive more nourishment than the disease can destroy, which means frequent feedings with highly concentrated food that is easily digested.

The best mixture consists of meat baby food and enough warm water to make the food soupy so that it will be easy to feed to the cat. Add about three drops of brandy to four teaspoonfuls of water. If the cat vomits the mixture, rest him for about half an hour and then feed again. You must persist in this feeding, as it is essential to the cat's recovery.

The cat must be confined to one room and kept warm and dry. His eyes, nose, and rear end must be cleaned often; this is best done with a cloth or a paper handkerchief and Q-Tips slightly moistened with olive or mineral oil. The bedding must be changed as soon as it is soiled, which may happen often because the diarrhea is sometimes extreme. The bedding should be burned.

If the veterinarian prescribes an eye medicine or an inhalant, well and good. If he does not, it is important that no home remedies be used.

The cat should not be allowed to creep into a dark corner and hide, because that way cats give up and die. On the other hand, he must not be exposed to a glaring light, which will hurt his eyes and make his headache worse.

Anyone who is nursing a cat with enteritis must keep away from other cats. Whether the cat survives or not, it is not proper to go near another cat for at least one month. No new cat should be brought into the house for at least a month after the end of the illness unless he has been immunized, and even then I would not be in a hurry.

Everything the sick cat has touched must be burned or otherwise disposed of in such a way that other cats cannot come into contact with it and catch enteritis. Since it isn't practical to destroy a house, or even a room, the cat's quarters must be scrubbed with a strong antiseptic solution and unvaccinated cats kept out of them for at least one month. It would be wise to use an antiviral aerosol spray or, if possible, a germicidal lamp.

FELINE INFECTIOUS ANEMIA

This disease is caused by a microscopic parasite that attacks the cat's red blood cells and destroys them. As a result, the cat becomes depressed and feverish, loses his appetite, shows signs of progressive anemia (such as lighter color of tongue and gums), eventually becomes emaciated, and may develop jaundice (yellow coloring of skin, gums, and so on). The exact method of transmission is not known, but most authorities believe that it is transferred by flea bites and cat-fight bites. Also, it appears that kittens may get the infection from an infected mother cat while still in the womb. The latest stages of this disease often look like cat enteritis. Your veterinarian should be the one to make the differential diagnosis and advise the proper treatment. The treatment for this condition may need to go on for weeks. Forced feeding, as in feline enteritis, is often necessary.

Some cats remain carriers of this disease even after they look completely cured. Therefore, a recovered cat should have a blood test for this infection every two or three months for at least one year after recovery. The owner of such a cat should always look for signs of the return of the disease—especially paleness of the tongue, nail sheaths, nose, gums. At present there is no vaccination against feline infectious anemia.

RABIES

People who live with cats need not worry too much about rabies. This disease cannot arise spontaneously. It can be transmitted only by an animal afflicted with the disease. It is contracted through a lesion in the skin from a bite or the saliva of a rabid animal. The principal animals that get rabies are dogs, foxes, wolves, rabbits, squirrels, bats, cows, horses. One of these animals, or any other species subject to rabies, would have to have rabies itself before it could possibly give rabies to your cat.

Great Britain, Denmark, Sweden, Norway, the Netherlands, Belgium, and Switzerland have eliminated rabies entirely by enforcing rigid quarantine on the entry of dogs. Quarantine and vaccination, properly enforced, would eliminate rabies here as well, and we would have no more rabies and no more rabies scares.

There is a special vaccine to protect cats against rabies. However, if your cat always stays in your own home and does not come into contact with other animals, there is no chance of his getting rabies and the vaccine is not necessary. If you travel with the cat or the cat goes outdoors, it is advisable to vaccinate.

Rabies can be diagnosed only by inoculation of laboratory animals with material taken from the brain of the suspected creature, or by post-mortem microscopic examination, and even that can be misleading. Any diagnosis based on other evidence is unreliable. Fits must not be confused with rabies. Shock, fright, hysteria, bellyache, injuries, and worms are much more likely to cause fits in any animal than rabies. Fits are not contagious or infectious.

Symptoms of cat rabies: Some cats may be friendly at the outset of the disease, but most cats show furious symptoms at the very start. They bite and scratch viciously. Or a cat may have the dumb form of rabies in which he just becomes quieter and weaker and does not attempt to bite, scratch, or show any other excitable symptoms.

FELINE INFECTIOUS CONJUNCTIVITIS

This condition is caused by a virus-like disease agent. It may occur in an acute or a chronic form. In the acute form, one eye only is infected. This eye is sensitive to light and the conjunctiva (membrane over the eyeball) is red and swollen and emits pus. If this eye is not treated, the other will become infected, usually within seven days.

In the chronic form, both eyes are affected and there is much less discharge. However, the conjunctivae are thicker and more inflamed.

Infected cats sometimes develop a watery nose discharge and sneeze at times.

If a mother cat has the disease, her kittens' eyes will often share the symptoms at the time their eyes open, when they are about ten days old. This may happen even when the mother cat has apparently recovered from the disease.

Needless to say, this condition requires immediate treatment. Antibiotics, locally and systemically used, have been very helpful. In some cases, cortisone derivatives have been used with success.

FELINE PERITRITIS

The exact cause of this disease is not known, but is believed to be a virus. The main symptoms are poor appetite, dullness, fever, and a swelling of the belly due to the formation of a thick, infected liquid in the peritoneal cavity. It generally affects cats from 3½ months to 3 years of age and may produce vomiting, diarrhea, yellow gums, and difficult breathing.

FELINE RESPIRATORY DISEASES

This is a very complicated subject on which we have had a lot of scientific research, but it requires much more. More than twenty cat respiratory viruses have been isolated up to this time.

Symptoms: Sneezing, coughing, running eyes, headache, depression, lowered appetite. Some are more severe and serious than others. If your cat shows any of these symptoms, you should immediately take him to a veterinarian for his advice and treatment.

The two most important respiratory viruses are feline pneumonitis and feline rhinotracheitis. Pneumonitis, which occurs in cats of all ages, even those fourteen years of age or more, is milder and much less deadly. In recovered cats, severe infection of the sinuses of the head often results, so that the cat has a chronic nasal discharge and recurrent headaches. The cat may get some relief, in such cases, if you swab his nostrils with Boroleum. Use it at the end of a Q-Tip. Also, you should discuss the use of nose drops (watery type) with your veterinarian. The cat often temporarily loses his sense of smell. In such a case, force-feed as described for FELINE ENTERITIS.

Another specific respiratory disease is feline influenza. This condition is also caused by a virus and resembles rhinotracheitis, but is not as highly contagious. In influenza, most cats develop lung trouble, diarrhea, and tongue sores (which lead to a lot of salivation). The treatment is similar to that of other respiratory diseases.

At present, there is a vaccine against pneumonitis but there are none against any of the other cat respiratory diseases. Further, one attack of pneumonitis does not make the cat immune indefinitely. Therefore, it is best to have your cat vaccinated against pneumonitis every six months. You can hope, with this method, for some immunity against some of the other respiratory viruses besides pneumonitis.

However, you should realize how complex this subject of cat respiratory diseases is. It may happen that although you have had your cat vaccinated against pneumonitis, he later does develop a respiratory disease. It would not be fair to blame the manufacturer of the vaccine, or the veterinarian, for your cat's illness.

KIDNEY AND BLADDER STONES

(Urinary Calculi)

In cats these are nearly always stones that have formed in the bladder, although some may have started to form in the kidney and worked down into the bladder or the urethra, where they stop the flow of urine by blocking the passage. Some of these are cheesy plugs rather than stones. The type of calculi will vary from cat to cat, one having stones, another gravel, and another the cheesy plugs; the last are the easiest to eliminate, as they are not hard.

Urinary calculi afflict cats of all ages. The trouble is that this condition sneaks up on the cat slowly and the symptoms may not be noticed until the cat has uremic poisoning, and then there is no hope. If caught in the early stages, it can sometimes be arrested and rearrested until the cat dies of old age. The way to catch it in time is to know the symptoms and start watching for them while the cat is still relatively young.

The first symptom to watch for is restlessness. If you do not know exactly why the cat is restless, it would be wise to take

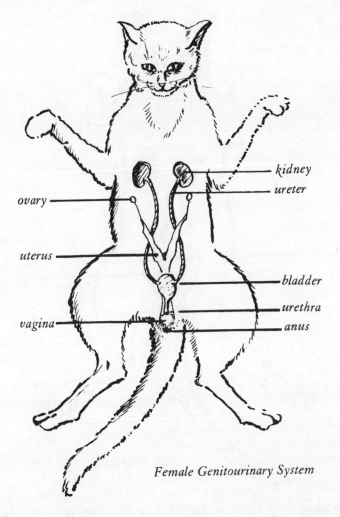

ovary

kidney

ureter

uterus

bladder

urethra

vagina

anus

Female Genitourinary System

him to the doctor. If it is a case of urinary stones, neglect will lead to a very serious condition rather than the mild one that the cat starts with.

The urethra is the tube that conveys the urine from the bladder to the outside. Particularly in a male cat, it may become

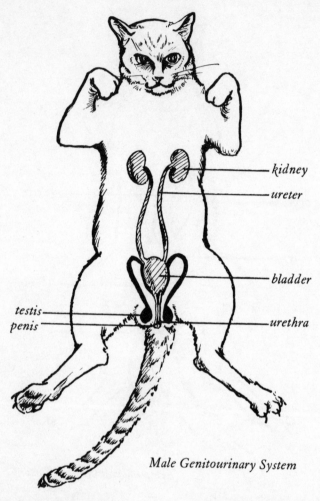

kidney
ureter
bladder
testis
penis
urethra

Male Genitourinary System

plugged up by a stone so that little or no urine will pass out. (The urethra of the female cat is much larger than that of the male. As a result, stones that would plug up the male's urethra will easily pass out of the female urethra without causing any trouble.) You may notice the cat's belly swelling. Do not be misled into thinking that this is a case of excess fat or constipation. People often give laxatives at this stage. You should instead allow your veterinarian to diagnose the condition and prescribe the proper treatment.

If you watch the cat try to urinate you will notice that the urine, if it comes out at all, does not come out in its regular stream-like form. Rather, the cat squats and strains and little drops of urine come out. These often are bloody. If so, the cat's bladder is probably seriously damaged. The cat may cry in pain when he urinates, and he may wet in the house outside of his pan. Some cats with this affliction become very thirsty; others may vomit.

The exact cause of this condition is still unknown. Foods, water, chemicals, fright, change of residence, infection, and other factors have all been implicated. The latest research points to a virus as the cause.

FITS

Shock, fright, hysteria, bellyache, injuries, worms, a bone in the throat or stomach, poisoning, exhaustion, cold food, and hot weather are some of the things that can give cats fits.

A fit may come on gradually or suddenly. The cat may shake all over or fall down and claw the air and twitch. He may screech or he may have a silent fit. He may foam at the mouth or he may not. The main thing to remember when a cat loses his wits is that you mustn't lose yours.

A cat in a fit may scratch or bite because he doesn't know what he is doing. Those scratches or bites are unintentional and no more dangerous than scratches or bites you might get while playing with the cat. A cat does not become poisonous or rabid just because he is having convulsions.

The first thing to do when a cat has a fit is to drop a heavy coat or blanket over him, roll it up, and wait for Puss to calm down.

If you are sure overheating in the sun caused the fit, take the kitten, or cat, out of the sun at once and put cold packs on his head. Then send for the veterinarian. It may even be necessary to immerse the cat up to his neck in cool—not cold—water until he quiets down. If this is resorted to, be sure to dry the cat thoroughly.

HEAT PROSTRATION

Old cats and fat cats are especially subject to heat prostration. Cats in good condition usually find cool spots to lie down in, keep out of the sun, and take it easy and are unperturbed by hot weather. Kittens seldom are prostrated unless they play too long in the sun.

Prostration is literally that: the cat collapses and is either unconscious or semiconscious. He is in no danger of having a fit and need not be handled cautiously or locked up. He does need a veterinarian immediately and urgently. Until you get the cat to your veterinarian, massage his chest very gently.

REPRODUCTIVE ORGANS

PERIODS OF HEAT

(Estrus)

The modern female cat does not seem to heed the advice of books which state she should have periods starting at about eight months of age and recurring about every three months thereafter. Cats vary tremendously nowadays. Some have their first period as early as at four months. Some cats have a period every week or so. The period may last one day and recur a few days later. It may last a week or more.

During the period, the cat will "call," elevate her hind legs with the front part of the body crouched down, roll around a lot, and rub against people and objects much more than usual. The "calling" may become very loud and extensive, especially at night, when reasonable humans want to sleep. The owner then has several alternatives: give the cat a tranquilizer or a sedative—ditto for the owner (and the neighbors may need the same); have the cat spayed; or have your veterinarian give her hormone injections. Before doing the last, make sure you know all about the risks involved in such an injection.

WOMB INFECTION

(Metritis—Pyometra)

In this condition, pus accumulates in the womb and causes it to swell. The exact cause is not always known, but factors are hormone abnormality, infection transported from other body organs, and infection from the outside of the vagina.

At the start of this condition your cat may show very little in the way of symptoms. She may be a little dull, a little thirstier than usual; her belly may swell up; she may eat less and vomit. Also, there may be a yellow, brown, or red discharge from the vagina, and the urinary system may become involved. Treatment may alleviate the symptoms for an indefinite period of time, but cats with pyometra can generally be cured permanently only by spaying.

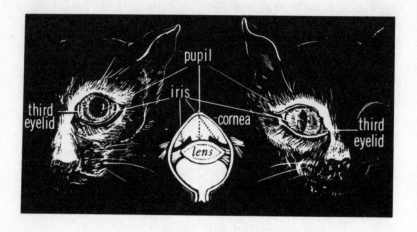

EYE TROUBLE

CONJUNCTIVITIS

This is an inflammation of the inner lining of the eyelid and transparent covering over the eyeball. It may be caused by foreign bodies, dust, injury, or infection. The eyes are red and watery and the third eyelid shows at the corners. Keep the eye clean through use of sterile cotton and boiled water. Apply a cardboard Elizabethan collar (see illustration on page 123). If improvement has not taken place in two or three days, take the cat to your veterinarian. (See also INFECTIOUS CONJUNCTIVITIS.)

KERATITIS

This is an inflammation of the outer layer of the eyeball. It is caused by accidental injury (city cats sometimes scratch their eyes on grass or briars when they first go to the country), wounds received in battle, or infections transported from other organs. The eyeball has a blue-white, clouded look. This condition requires professional treatment.

CORNEAL ULCER

Causes: Generally, injury to the eye followed by infection. It may also be caused by a tumor or cut on the eyelid, folding in of the eyelid, or curled-in hairs on the eyelid.

Symptoms: Blinking of eyes, sensitivity to light, damage to eyeball. The damage may be so slight at the start that you do not suspect anything serious. If the condition is permitted to continue, permanent scarring of the eyeball often occurs even if belated treatment is administered. The ulcer may start as a slight scratch on the eyeball which can be seen only in a strong light. As the disease progresses the lesion goes deeper into the eyeball and eventually a hole forms in the eyeball. Therefore, it is best to take the cat to your veterinarian as soon as any eye trouble appears.

CATARACT

This condition is most common in old cats. However, young cats may develop it too, and some cats are born with it. Cataract is less noticeable than keratitis and much more serious. It is an opacity of the lens of the eye. No one knows the exact cause of cataract. It is generally believed that no medication will alleviate cataract, but an operation can be performed to remove the opaque lens. Even this is not advisable unless the cataract is ripe (completely opaque) and the cat is fairly young. Cataracts often do not start until the cat is eight to ten years old, and usually he will die of old age or some other cause before he goes completely blind as a result of cataract. Therefore, you should not be alarmed about this condition, and you should weigh alternatives before doing anything radical.

POISONING

INTRODUCTION

If you suspect that a cat has been poisoned, get him to the nearest veterinarian immediately. If you cannot, try the first-aid treatment described in the following paragraphs.

First-aid treatment varies with the poison. In most (not all) cases of poisoning by mouth, you should try to make the cat vomit if: (1) he has not already vomited, (2) he is conscious, and (3) a short time has passed since he ate the poison. To induce vomiting: First, try to get a teaspoonful of pure table salt on the back of the cat's tongue. If you cannot do this, dissolve two teaspoonfuls of salt in six ounces of warm water and administer to the cat as described under HOW TO GIVE A CAT LIQUID MEDICINE.

A mixture that can be used as a universal antidote for various types of poison consists of one tablespoonful of strong tea, one teaspoonful of milk of magnesia, and two teaspoonfuls of pulverized burned toast. You should use this only if you cannot get a veterinarian's assistance. Further, you should always try to make the cat vomit before using the mixture.

Recent investigation at the University of Arizona shows that evaporated milk is fairly effective in preventing absorption from the stomach and intestines. Therefore, you should try some evaporated milk after the previous mixture has been used.

In many cases of cat poisoning a tranquilizer or sedative is required. It would be wise to keep some on hand at all times; ask your veterinarian for a prescription, together with proper dosage.

If the cat has come into contact with poison via the skin,

wash the skin with plenty of warm water and soap. If the poison was inhaled, make sure that the cat gets plenty of fresh air.

ARSENIC POISONING

Arsenic is used in roach and rat poisons. Small amounts may be contained in some human medicines. Cats can ingest arsenic by eating arsenic-poisoned mice or eating poisoned food put out for mice.

The symptoms of arsenic poisoning are abdominal cramps; extreme thirst; vomiting; bloody diarrhea; fast, shallow breathing; exhaustion; then complete collapse.

Arsenic poisoning is sometimes mistaken for gastroenteritis, and vice versa. In either case you call the vet as quickly as you humanly can.

Then, if you know the cat may have had access to arsenic, put half a teaspoonful of salt on the back of his tongue to make him vomit. After the cat vomits, give him a little Kaopectate; this is to ease the abdominal pain until the doctor comes.

If the cat is unconscious, don't try to give him anything; just wait for the veterinarian, and hope.

ASPIRIN POISONING

Be very cautious about giving aspirin to your cat. Even small doses, such as two grains a day, have caused the following symptoms in cats: depression, poor appetite, vomiting, and sometimes convulsions. Doses of five grains a day (the common human aspirin tablet) have caused destruction of the liver, stomach damage, and lowering of the number of red cells in the blood. I would advise that you never give aspirin to your cat unless it is specifically prescribed.

CARBOLIC POISONING

Cats are highly susceptible to carbolic acid poisoning. A great many cats are poisoned by it because their people don't know what contains carbolic acid and what does not.

The technically correct name of carbolic acid is phenol. It is obtained by distillation of coal gas. Many household disinfectants contain carbolic acid, which, even greatly diluted, will kill a cat.

The symptoms of phenol poisoning are similar to those of paint and arsenic poisoning. The difference is that the cat's breath probably will smell of carbolic acid, Lysol, or whatever form of phenol poisoned him. Vomiting, diarrhea, gasping, and shivering are characteristic.

Give the cat as much milk of magnesia as you can get into him—a tablespoonful or more won't hurt under the circumstances. Just be sure not to choke him. Milk of magnesia is an antidote as well as a purgative in this case; use it as such.

If the cat is very weak, but conscious, feed him a little strong, cool, black coffee.

The rest is up to the veterinarian.

CHLORDANE POISONING

You should not use any flea killer on a cat except one containing pyrethrum or rotenone or derivative as the active ingredient (read the label of the can you are using). If your cat does get chlordane poisoning, you may note that he will salivate excessively, develop severe diarrhea, and go into convulsions. If you cannot get him to your veterinarian immediately, it is essential that you try to sedate or tranquilize the cat. You should then immediately wash the cat with warm soapy water, rinse thoroughly, and dry well.

GAS POISONING

Cooking gas, coal gas, and carbon monoxide can poison cats as well as people. You should never leave a cat alone in a room with a gas stove, or any other gas outlet, unless the gas source is locked in some way. If there isn't a lock, have a carpenter or plumber make one. A cat fooling around a gas stove can blow up the house and kill everybody.

A cat with gas poisoning gasps for breath and shivers; his gums and eyeballs are bluish; his temperature is subnormal; and he may have convulsions.

The remedy is to get the cat outdoors at once and apply artificial respiration. Lay the cat on an old coat or any soft thing that will raise his middle a bit higher than his head. Turn the cat's head to one side so that he can breathe. Then, kneeling behind the cat, place both hands over his lower ribs and push, slowly, firmly toward the head. Count eight and release the pressure. Count eight and repeat. Continue until the cat begins to breathe. If the cat does not respond in a couple of minutes, send for the veterinarian. Hold aromatic spirits of ammonia or any other smelling salts to the cat's nose every few minutes until he becomes conscious. Don't give up hope for at least half an hour.

At this point, let me advise you to keep a small oxygen tank in your home for both cats and people. It usually costs about $8 at your druggist's and may save someone's life. It would certainly help your cat if he should get gas poisoning or need oxygen during an illness such as pneumonia or a heart attack. This type of oxygen tank is very simple to use. It is packed with a plastic mask, and you need merely push a button to administer the oxygen to your cat.

PAINT POISONING

Cats sometimes get lead poisoning from licking paint off various places, from drinking out of old paint cans, or even from paint fumes if they are shut up in an apartment that is being painted.

If you are sure the poisoning was caused only by inhalation of paint fumes, get the cat away from the place being painted and into one with plenty of fresh air. Watch him closely. If the cat isn't well in an hour, or if he has licked paint, send for the veterinarian.

The symptoms of paint poisoning are just like those of arsenic poisoning.

Give the cat two teaspoonfuls of Epsom salts in a little warm water. Beat up the white of an egg in milk and feed this to the cat.

If the cat is very weak, a little strong, black coffee may help him.

PHOSPHORUS POISONING

Phosphorus is the killing ingredient in some paste poisons put out for roaches, which plague all city people no matter how clean they are. Cats seldom eat the stuff, but they may step in it and then lick it off their feet, which is the same thing in the long run.

Phosphorus poisoning works slowly. Several days may pass between the time the cat swallows phosphorus and the time he becomes seriously ill.

The symptoms are greenish-brown vomit, restlessness, abdominal cramps, and weakness. The cat's tongue swells; his gums and eyeballs are yellowish, as if he had jaundice. His breath usually smells of phosphorus.

Give the cat two teaspoonfuls or tablets of milk of magnesia or Epsom salts.

Never give a cat oil of any kind when phosphorus poisoning is suspected.

Mix half a teaspoonful of flour with an equal amount of water and feed this to the cat in the hope that it may absorb some of the phosphorus-poisoned material inside the cat.

Do not give the cat any food before the veterinarian sees him.

PLANT POISONING

There are a number of plants that are highly toxic to cats. They include philodendron, large-leaf ivies, sheep laurel, and mountain laurel. Various symptoms of plant poisoning are dullness, weakness, excessive salivation, running eyes, paralysis. The amount of damage to the cat depends on the amount of the plant eaten and the power of the poison in the particular plant. To satisfy your cat's hunger for fresh greens, I would advise that you get oat seeds and grow pots of oats in your house. For first aid see the introduction on poisons.

STRYCHNINE POISONING

Strychnine is a swift and terrible poison. Very few cats survive even the smallest trace of it. People may—as mentioned above—kill their own cats by ignorantly giving them overdoses of cathartics, prepared for humans, that contain small amounts of strychnine. Also, strychnine is used in some roach powders. If a cat steps into even a small amount of strychnine-poisoned powder and then licks it off his foot, he may die.

The symptoms come swiftly and hit hard. First the cat begins to shake and twitch. At this point you call the veterinarian. If you cannot see him very quickly, try to make the cat vomit (see procedure under FOREIGN BODIES). The moment the cat has vomited, give him another dose.

If the twitching has not eased considerably within ten minutes, give the cat a sedative. You should powder the sedative tablet, dilute it with water, and use a teaspoon or plastic eye dropper to insert it in the side of the cat's mouth. If the twitching increases and becomes convulsive jerks, give the cat more sedative. This is done in order to prevent convulsions.

Don't be too frightened if the cat becomes partially or completely paralyzed. His eyes may bulge, his jaws clench (that's why you need to get the vomiting over and the medicine down quickly), and his head and tail may bend upward in a peculiar and dreadful way. A cat can survive all that.

Keep a blanket handy to throw over the cat in case he suffers convulsions before help arrives.

Don't worry if the cat becomes unconscious. Keep him warm. It is necessary that the cat be quieted down, as continuous convulsions would surely mean the death of the cat.

THALLIUM POISONING

This chemical is used in rat and mouse poisons. Thallium poisoning causes reddening and crusting of the skin, especially near the body openings, followed by baldness. Other symptoms are thirst, diarrhea, vomiting, dullness, weakness, and sometimes fits. Most cats die ten to fourteen days after being poisoned. As there is no effective antidote, treatment is best left to your veterinarian. If this is not possible, use evaporated milk and baby food to force-feed the cat.

SNAKE BITE

Snake bite is an occupational hazard of cats that live in snake-infested country. People who live with cats in snaky surroundings should keep snake-bite serum on hand at all times. You can't tell who might need it. Be sure you find out how much each pet animal on the place should be given and how to administer the dose if it should be needed. Cats rid the world of a great many poisonous snakes—copperheads and rattlesnakes in the North; rattlers, coral snakes, and cottonmouth moccasins in the South—and the least we can do is be prepared to take care of them in case a snake strikes back.

A cat is usually bitten in the face or forelegs while killing a snake, though a big rattler may thrash loose and bite farther back.

The first symptoms are swelling with two small punctures caused by the snake's fangs. The cat vomits, breathes with great difficulty, and is extremely weak.

First—with another person holding the cat in a heavy towel or blanket—you inject the snake-bite serum as directed. Then you call the veterinarian. Next you slash the swelling deeply several times with a knife or razor blade and squeeze out as much of the poison as you can. Don't be squeamish about slashing; or if you are, slash anyway. And don't be afraid of the venom; it can't harm you unless it gets into your blood, which it can't do unless your skin is broken. Wear rubber gloves if you can.

If the cat was bitten on a leg, put a tourniquet above the bite, between the bite and the cat's heart, and make it very tight. If you possibly can, hold the cat so that a stream of tepid water flows constantly over the slashes and washes out the venom.

FIRST AID FOR INJURIES

CUTS

Slight cuts should be washed well with soap and water and made to bleed if they will; after that they should take care of themselves. If inflammation should develop, apply a hot, wet compress every hour until the wound opens, and after that several times a day. A slight cut is not likely to cause trouble.

If the cut is medium deep, clip the hair from around it and wash it thoroughly. Then take your cat to the veterinarian.

If the cut is deep and bleeding profusely, don't bother with soap and water. Quickly put a big wad of gauze and cotton over the wound, tie it tight enough to slow up the bleeding, and rush the cat to the veterinarian. In case the injury is on a leg or foot, fasten a tourniquet between the cut and the cat's heart, and hurry to the doctor. You can make a tourniquet out of any cloth, including a dishrag or a tie, that will wrap around the leg and tie in a double knot. Stick a pencil or anything of the sort through the knot, twist it tight, and there's your tourniquet. If it must be kept on for any length of time, release the pressure every ten minutes or so for a few seconds; then if the cut still bleeds, tighten it again.

DOG BITES

Dogs sometimes maul cats frightfully. First aid as outlined above should be applied at once. If the dog was known to be in good health when it bit the cat, there is no need to worry about rabies. If the dog was unknown—a stray, perhaps—or is suspected of being rabid, that fact should be reported to the veterinarian as a matter of form.

CAT BITES AND SCRATCHES

Cat bites and scratches are the inevitable result of cat fights. Trivial scratches need no attention, especially if the cat can lick them clean.

Severe lacerations should receive the same treatment as cuts.

Whenever a cat comes home from the wars, he should be looked over for wounds, and any lesion that cuts through the skin should be thoroughly washed with soap and water. You should watch your cat, carefully, for at least a week after he has been bitten. An abscess may form under the skin and show very little outward trouble.

RAT BITES

Rat bites are dangerous. Rats are filthy things with dirty teeth, and the bites they inflict on cats often become infected because they jab through the flesh rather than tear, as cat and dog bites do. The wound is often small but deep, with a tendency to heal first on the outside. This encapsulates dirt, cat hair, or any other source of infection inside the cat, and an abscess may form. Rat-bite abscesses are serious infections and sometimes kill cats. Prompt and efficient first aid will prevent them from developing.

Cats are nearly always bitten in the face by rats trying to struggle free. Any squarish, chisel-shaped cut on a cat's face, neck, or shoulders should be regarded as a rat bite and treated accordingly.

The best thing to do is clip the skin around the bite and clean it thoroughly with soap and water. Then flood the cut with hot water. Don't bandage it. Keep the cat indoors for three or four days, and wash the wound with hot water twice a day. Make sure it heals from the inside out. If in spite of your care a swelling develops, take Puss to your veterinarian.

For all their agility and skill, cats fall out of windows, stick their paws in traps, and hurt their tails in closing doors. Many cats have broken tails because they were too dignified or too lazy to go through doors faster than careless people closed them.

If the cat's tail is merely bruised, let it alone; the cat will take care of it. If the skin is broken, treat it like any other cut. If the tail is broken, it should be set.

Other broken bones are more serious. They must be set by the veterinarian, and I think you'd better let him find them, too. A cat with a broken bone either refuses to move at all or limps painfully. If you have reason to suspect that the cat may have a broken bone, put him in his traveling basket. or a ventilated box, handling him as little as possible, and take him to the doctor.

It is not true that cats always land on their feet. The fall may be so short that the cat has no space in which to turn, or some obstacle may break his fall in the middle of the turn. The cat may be stunned before he falls and unable to right himself. Also, the fall may be so great that the cat's landing on his feet doesn't help. He may fall three stories and hardly get hurt. He may fall from a chair and break one or more bones.

In addition to broken bones, a cat may be internally injured by a fall. A cat knows about broken bones at once. He may show no sign of internal injury for hours and then become seriously ill.

If the cat shows no symptoms, he should be kept in the house, preferably in one room, for three days. Don't fuss over the cat or encourage him to play during that time. Don't feed the cat anything at all the first twenty-four hours. If at the end of the twenty-four hours the cat isn't hungry, you'd better call the veterinarian. If the cat is hungry, give him a small portion of food at a time. Keep him on half rations during the period of observation.

AUTO ACCIDENTS

If a cat struck by a car is not killed outright, the injury nevertheless is usually serious. Whether it looks serious or not, you should take him to the veterinarian immediately because there may be internal injuries.

BURNS

It may be true that any cat which has once jumped on a hot stove will never again jump on any stove, but many cats do it once. Besides, there are other ways of getting burned.

Never use any patent burn reliever on a cat unless you are absolutely certain it can't harm him. Many burn salves contain small amounts of carbolic acid, enough to kill a cat.

If the cat burns himself slightly, apply a compress saturated with super-strong tea or with baking-soda solution (a handful of soda to half a cupful of warm water). Later, white Vaseline will ease the soreness.

If a large part of the cat's body is burned, you'll have to take him to the doctor. But first, and immediately, cover the burn completely with Vaseline.

The new antibiotic ointments will help prevent infections from burns. Any good vitamin A and D ointment will help stimulate healing. Sulfamylon cream is excellent for burns.

RICKETS

Rickets is an abnormal development of the bones in growing kittens that didn't get, or couldn't assimilate, enough calcium and phosphorus.

Found kittens often have rickets. The symptoms are fairly easy to recognize: The cat's forelegs are short and bowed. The wrist joints are enlarged, and there may be cartilaginous lumps, like small beads, along the junction of the ribs. The cat's coat is dull; it is generally thin and flabby.

Good food and some supplementary calcium, phosphorus, and vitamins will help the patient. Your veterinarian will advise you about proper care.

BRITTLE BONES

(Osteogenesis Imperfecta)
(Nutritional Secondary Hypoparathyroidism)

Brittle bones (Osteogenesis imperfecta) is thought to be a calcium-deficiency condition. If a cat does not get enough calcium, the parathyroid (a gland in the body) tries to draw calcium from all parts of the body and especially from the marrow (soft inside part) of the bones. This results in a wide marrow and a thin shell (the actual bone matter) around the marrow.

The bone becomes very fragile and is easily fractured. This occurs mostly in young kittens. There may be lameness, dullness, and, later, sensitivity to handling, hysteria, and convulsions. The hindquarters are especially affected, and the kitten may be unable to stand. Constipation often results as the pelvic

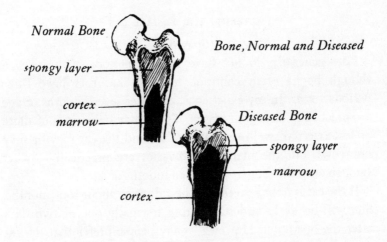

Normal Bone

spongy layer

cortex

marrow

Bone, Normal and Diseased

Diseased Bone

spongy layer

marrow

cortex

girdle (through which the rectum passes) becomes narrow. A female cat with this condition should not be bred, as it may be impossible for the kittens to pass through the pelvic canal. It is best to have a veterinarian give a cat the indicated injections and prescribe the proper medicine.

This condition very frequently occurs in kittens that are fed exclusively on a meat-and-water diet. I recommend the addition of a high-quality cat food such as CD to the raw meat. The kitten should be taught to eat CD at an early age—six weeks old if possible. CD is obtainable through your veterinarian.

OPTIONAL OPERATIONS

There are certain operations pertaining to a cat which you may or may not wish to have performed. It is important that you know the facts about them so that you can decide what is best for you and your own cat.

ALTERING THE FEMALE CAT

(Spaying)

Cats generally do not have regular periods of heat, even though books often continue to state that cats have three periods a year. In my experience, cats over seven months of age are practically always in season. There may be periods of more or less external swelling of the vulva, and the cat may or may not yowl, but the uterus and ovaries are practically always swollen once the cat gets past seven months of age.

If the cat is to be spayed, it is best done at about four months. She will be lively and start eating normally one or two days after the operation. However, many people prefer that the cat develop to maturity, about six to seven months of age, before spaying, and the exact age depends on the wishes of the individual. However, if you do wait longer to have the cat spayed, you should be ready to put up with sleepless nights and irate neighbors, especially if you live in a city apartment. The cries of a cat during the height of her period ring loud and clear, especially if she is a Siamese or Burmese.

Sometimes you may wish to have your cat spayed after she has developed to maturity and practically always shows signs of strong heat. An operation at this time would be riskier than the spaying of a younger cat. Therefore, you should ask your veterinarian about giving your cat a hormone injection which will prevent a period for at least a month. This will give the swollen organs a chance to reduce in size. Then the cat can be spayed at smaller risk. However, you should realize that there is risk in giving the hormone injection, and you must make sure to have the cat spayed once you have given her the hormone injection.

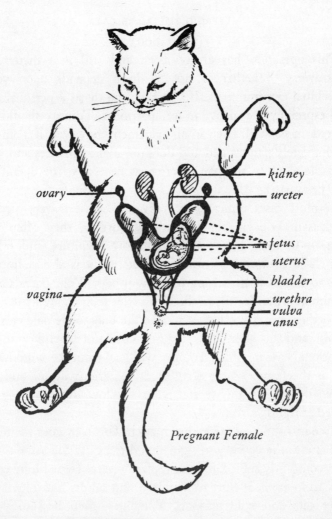

ovary

kidney
ureter

fetus
uterus
bladder
vagina
urethra
vulva
anus

Pregnant Female

If you do not have your cat spayed, be sure that she has several litters of kittens during her first six years of life. Otherwise, she will be more more prone to breast and womb trouble later in life.

ALTERING THE MALE CAT
(Castration)

This operation has always been and still is a matter of controversy. Whether or not to do it depends upon your individual circumstances. If you keep the cat as a personal pet and especially if you live in an apartment, Tommy should be altered, in general. Even in an apartment, however, if Tommy is completely pan-trained and does not make mistakes and you are able to clean the pan as often as necessary, the operation may be averted.

In most cases tomcats do spray and cause a very strong unpleasant odor in the apartment. Further, they often are unclean in their habits and will spray furniture and other household equipment, with the result that it is almost impossible to eliminate the strong unpleasant odor. Your friends and neighbors will inform you about this odor soon enough.

Further, the city cat does receive the odor of female cats in season, and this often leads to a fine session of yowling plus an occasional case in which Tommy will leap from the window to get at the female. This often leads to serious injury and, at times, death. For this reason, your windows must always be closed or tightly screened.

A country tomcat is another matter. This tom goes roaming and enjoys the country air, grass, and trees. At the same time, he is constantly subject to injury, often severe. He is hit by cars, falls from trees, is hurt by children and adults and bitten by other cats and wild animals. The bites often lead to deep abscesses which can become very serious if not treated promptly and properly. You should consider all these matters carefully before deciding whether or not to have your cat neutered.

Many altered cats do get fat and lazy, but this does not necessarily happen. Much of this is controlled by the owner. You must make sure that the food you serve is lower in calories. There is no doubt that an altered cat's metabolism is much more efficient than that of an unaltered cat; in other words, the altered cat's body makes better use of food. However, the owner can feed fewer calories to his cat and keep the cat's weight down; this will prevent the undesirable laziness and slothfulness.

Another controversial facet is that of urinary stones and urethral obstruction. The latest research on this condition was reported in the April 1968 *Journal of Small Animal Proceedings*. Essential abstracts from this article state that "There did not appear to be any association of the onset of the condition with age of castration. The ratio of castration to uncastrated cats getting urinary obstruction is the same as the normal cat population." From this research we can see that there does not seem to be any difference between tomcats and altered cats. Further, other research has shown that castration does not produce constriction of the urethra. Therefore, I feel a tomcat should be altered before he matures.

DECLAWING

Until about ten years ago this subject was practically taboo. One would hardly discuss the subject, much less do the operation. We now know that if it is done properly the cat does not in most cases suffer unduly. It is best done at an early age— about three months. At this age the cat is incapacitated only one to seven days. However, declawing can be done at any age. It has been done in twelve-year-old cats with good results. After his paws are healed, Puss should be able to flex them as usual and climb. However, the operation should not be done on a cat that lives outside or in the country or any cat that needs to defend itself.

YELLOW FAT

(Steatitis)
(Vitamin E Deficiency)

In the past this was a very common disease and was generally caused by feeding of canned cat foods, especially tuna, that contained very little Vitamin E and a lot of highly unsaturated fatty acids. This was a dangerous combination and resulted in muscle weakness, liver damage, fetal absorption, and, ultimately, a change in the color of the body fat from white to yellow or even brown. To avoid this condition, you need only check the label of the canned food you use. Make sure it says "Vitamin E added." The manufacturers have learned the proper ratio of Vitamin E to add to unsaturated fatty acids, and use of their products will not cause yellow fat.

MOUTH AND LIPS

TOOTH TROUBLES

Kittens rarely have trouble teething. Well-fed kittens should have no difficulty at all. Even the urge to gnaw that strikes teething puppies seldom gets into kittens. If you have a runt kitten who seems healthy but scarcely grows at all, it would be wise to examine his teeth every week or so just to make sure they are growing properly.

Older cats are subject to toothache because their teeth (like ours, alas) decay and fall. Usually the little incisors are first to go, and they seem to vanish without disturbing the cat much. Other teeth may abscess and, if not attended to, will cause a great deal of trouble.

You should examine your cat's teeth at least once a month—all its life. If you see any deposits of yellow or greenish matter on the teeth, near the gum line particularly, have the teeth scraped. In most cats this can be done without anesthesia if the cat is gently handled. If the tartar is allowed to remain, the gum will separate from the teeth and infection will set in. This will produce a painful condition, even though many cats do not show it. If a tooth becomes infected it can sometimes be saved by proper treatment. If not, the tooth should be extracted. Otherwise, an infected tooth will affect the tooth next to it and that one the next, and so on until the cat, even at an early age, may lose all its teeth. Proper inspection and care will prevent this and avert painful experiences for the cat.

LIP ULCER

(Rodent Ulcer)

This is a sore on the lip that refuses to heal. If it is not cured, more and more of the lip is eroded until the full depth of the lip at the point of the ulcer has been eaten away and the gum and teeth are exposed. This condition should be treated by your veterinarian. Depending upon the severity of the condition, medical treatment, cauterization, X-ray, or surgery may be needed.

TONGUE ULCER

This is a persistent sore of the tongue which may be caused by infection, vitamin deficiency, bad teeth, or a combination of these. Treatment requires the services of a veterinarian.

JAW SWELLINGS

You should have these examined. They may be cysts, tumors, osteomyelitis, abscesses (and a sewing needle may be involved here). Most of these conditions require an operation of one type or another.

TONGUE CYST

You will see a soft bladder-like swelling on the underside of the tongue, and your cat will show distress in eating. This generally requires an operation.

SORE GUMS

(Red Gums)

You will note a dark red line near the teeth. This is a common condition in cats but is not completely understood. It may be due to poor nutrition, infection (local or general), vitamin deficiency, anemia, poor teeth, or a combination of these. Vitamin supplement, antibiotics, daily gum massage, and proper care of the teeth will alleviate this condition.

THE AGING CAT

Cats that have good care often live for a long time. Some have been known to live as long as twenty-five years. However, most cats do not live longer than twelve to fifteen years. A new diet helps to keep them young. There are medicines to help increase kidney functions and to stimulate old hearts and keep old blood circulating. Vitamin B complex stirs up tired digestions. Sex hormones restore lost youth.

You have to treat the symptoms one by one as they appear. I think it is advisable to take an elderly cat to the doctor once a year for a checkup, because the veterinarian can see trouble coming long before most people would notice anything wrong.

If his teeth are gone, you will have to grind his meat or feed him baby food. Otherwise you shouldn't make any change: the cat's stomach is set in its ways by now. And don't reduce the quantity of food unless the cat is very fat. Even then you have to consider whether old Puss would rather die happy or live longer but hungry.

Old cats may have strokes—one final stroke or a number of slight ones, each more crippling than the last. Also, an old cat may wake one morning to find that his legs don't work right; he stumbles or falls, and jumping into a chair is quite a job. This is usually caused by atrophy of the muscles due to old age.

WHAT YOU CAN CATCH FROM A CAT, AND WHAT A CAT CAN CATCH FROM YOU

There are very few ailments that people catch from cats; but you should be acquainted with those few even though this rarely happens. Mange is theoretically transmissible from cats to people, though it doesn't seem to happen very often.

Ringworm is promiscuous. The cat can get it from you, and you can get it from the cat. All of the fungus diseases are exchangeable.

It is remotely possible to get dog tapeworm from a cat. This tapeworm, *Dipylidium caninum,* spends part of its embryonic life in fleas or lice. Youthful dog fleas that haven't yet acquired the epicurean exclusiveness of their elders sometimes get onto cats. If a young dog flea carrying a load of *Dipylidium caninum* should happen to get on the cat, and you should happen to eat it, you might get tapeworm. I trust this won't worry you unduly.

Cat fleas sometimes get onto people, but they like cats better. However, fleas will hide in a dark corner of your home and jump on to people when cats are not handy.

If a cat should be bitten by a rabid dog and should contract the disease, which doesn't necessarily follow, and, while rabid, should bite you, you might get rabies.

People do not catch pneumonia, pleurisy, tuberculosis, the common cold, diphtheria, scarlet fever, whooping cough, mumps, measles, or any other human disease from cats.

WHEN THE CAT BITES YOU

Cat bites and scratches are neither more nor less dangerous than similar injuries received in any other way. If the cat's teeth and claws are clean, you are scratched and that is all. If they are dirty and the germs on them are bad for people, you may or may not be infected. Some people are infected by a pinprick; others are bitten, scratched, kicked, and butted without any consequences beyond temporary soreness and loss of temper.

HOW TO STOP A CAT FIGHT

The best way to stop a cat fight is to throw water on the fighters: cold water and plenty of it. Cold water will also make the neighbor's dog sorry he picked on your cat. Don't sail in and try to snatch your dear kitty from the jaws of death; not only are you likely to be bitten or scratched, you'll confuse your own cat and give the enemy an advantage. If you simply must rescue your cat, throw a blanket or coat over him before you try to remove him bodily.

DON'TS

Don't set up as an amateur diagnostician of feline ailments just because you guessed right once. Anybody can guess right once. If you guess wrong once, you may not have a cat to guess about.

Don't think that bottle of medicine you got when Fido was sick will cure the cat. It won't. Dogs can take with equanimity drugs that are fatal to cats. Even if the stuff is not by nature dangerous to cats, the dosages are different for dogs and cats.

Don't give the cat that laxative which worked wonders for Aunt Jenny. Many commercial laxatives prepared for people contain small amounts of strychnine. Strychnine in small amounts is deadly to cats.

Don't give a cat castor oil. It is too violent—too griping—and can actually be damaging. Besides, it is bad enough to be a sick cat without having to take castor oil too.

Don't use carbolic acid solutions or any carbolic derivative or any coal-tar disinfectant of any kind on or near a cat.

Don't wash a cat with medicated soap.

Don't use iodine on a cat unless it is recommended as a specific remedy.

Don't put iodine on any spot that the cat can possibly lick. If you must use iodine, be sure to hold the cat until the burning stops and the iodine is quite dry. There are other antiseptics, such as peroxide, and good old soap and water.

Don't ever use DDT, chlordane or any of the other new bug killers on a cat, near a cat, or even in a room to which a cat has access. They are wonderful vermin killers, and they will kill anything else that gets a sufficient dose. It isn't safe to let a cat into a room that was sprayed with DDT months ago unless the walls and floors have been thoroughly scrubbed, because DDT leaves a residue on anything it touches, and if a cat rubs against a DDT-coated surface and then licks his fur, that may be his last lick.

Don't touch sick cats away from home.

Don't touch other cats when your cat is sick.

Don't play with the animals in the vet's waiting room.

Don't tip a cat's head back when giving him liquid medicine. That is the way to strangulation.

Don't feed a cat hit-or-miss, or any old thing, and expect him to stay healthy.

Don't pick up a cat or a kitten by the scruff of the neck. You are not a mamma cat; you've got big, rough hands. A mamma cat knows exactly where to take hold of a kitten and exactly how tightly she should hold it; you don't. A cat more than a month old can actually be injured by such treatment. Its eyes may pop out of their sockets. Its insides may be displaced. And you might get scratched, which would serve you right.

XI

Dat Ole Debbil Sex

When archaeologists of some distant future civilization excavate the ruins of our cities they will be surprised to find that our back yards are composed ten per cent of earth and ninety per cent of broken pop bottles, and smashed electric bulbs, with a smattering of empty tin cans, ash trays, and old shoes. As a result of this discovery, the Twentieth Century probably will be known as "The Pop-Bottle Era of Machine-Age Culture," and learned treatises will be written to show that we Machine Agers worshiped the juke box and ceremonially smashed coke bottles to the tuneless hot licks of boogie-woogie. They'll never believe we spent our nights throwing things at lovelorn cats that dodged and went right on being lovelorn. Nor will they believe that the vocal aspect of the love life of cats was a major preoccupation of staid businessmen and immaculate matrons in this era of glorious gadgets. How can those future scientists understand that a nation which produced lady riveters and male crooners preferred the cacophony of jazz to the honest caterwauling that results in kittens?

The truth is we're envious. Our own love life is neurotic and frustrated almost to the point of race suicide; yet we say we like ourselves as we are and disapprove of cats because their sex life is forthright and uninhibited, which goodness knows it is. When the moon is high, cats are too. The rest of the time they'd rather have liver. This, from the cat's point of view, is as it should be. It leads to kittens and more kittens. Adolescence comes early to cats, and maturity lasts long. One cat in Ohio bore three hundred kittens in her lifetime, and cats with a hundred and fifty or two hundred kittens are nothing out of the ordinary.

People who live sensibly in the country needn't worry about the sex life of cats. Country cats go off and get some kittens, have them in the hay-mow, and their folks enjoy the delights of raising kittens.

City people who let cats out worry about them. City cats who aren't let out worry about themselves whenever they have sex on their minds.

Tomcats, in town or country, are no trouble at all if they can go outdoors for their toilet. Tomcats indoors are as decorous as cats with no sex at all—plainly they consider their private lives their own affair.

It is only when he is obliged to use a pan indoors that a tomcat poses a problem, as they say in books. When a male cat reaches sexual maturity his urine develops that unique and overpowering odor which is commonly called "cat smell." The cat himself does not smell even the least faint little bit—only his

All cats are potential alley cats

urine, which is the quintessence of stink. You can't wash cat smell away or deodorize it away or get rid of it by any manner of means. It pervades everything and after a while the whole house smells, your clothes smell—you smell.

This odor, believe it or not, is a form of advertising, the oldest in the world, I guess. It says plainer than any words dreamed up by $20,000-a-year copywriters that this is, "The reckless allure hidden in the sweet intimacy and lushness of the sultry night . . . redolent of dark, and mysterious charms in the aura of breathless beauty on the dewy, moon-bespattered back fence." In short, cat smell is the feline equivalent of *Chanel Number 5.*

When he's particularly eager to meet a personable young female, intention matrimony, a tomcat sprays whiffs of cat smell about in the hope of luring a maiden feline to his moon-bespattered lair. If he can't get out, he'll spray around the windows and doors. Female cats also spray. It doesn't smell so much and may not be noticed unless they learn to appreciate the wonders of electricity, as Spattie did. I thwarted Spattie's desire to express herself, and in her frustration she learned that by backing up to a light socket and spraying into it she could make a gratifying burst of flame shoot out. The resultant darkness and confusion didn't bother Spattie, but I soon realized that raising kittens would be a lot less bother than living with a cat in love with the Edison Company.

It is sometimes possible to let a tomcat go out and attend to his toilet and his love life from an upstairs city apartment. One cat I know owns a basket with bell and stout rope attached. When he wants to go out he jumps into the basket, paws the bell until it tinkles, and his people lower him to the garden, three stories down. When he's been out long enough Chips jumps into his basket, rings the bell, and is pulled up. Another tomcat I know solved the cat-pan problem for himself by using the toilet and pulling the chain. The average of cats and people is less ingenious than that, so most male cats that live in apartments are gelded when they grow up.

The idea of castrating a pet is revolting to any normal person, and it was only with the greatest difficulty that I forced myself to admit that some cats actually are improved by being neutered. Dr. Johnson has never observed any change in a cat's disposition after it had been unsexed. Since this is a psychological rather than a medical opinion, I feel free to disagree. It has been my observation that some cats grow fat and sluggish and good-for-nothing after castration. Some seem to be unchanged; I knew one cat who never seemed to realize he'd had an operation and continued to gallivant and fight as if nothing had happened. A few cats apparently divert the energy which would have been spent on caterwauling and kittens into deep devotion to people who played that dirty trick on them. Pickle, Charlie, Ben, Scoop, Kittenbum, and dozens of other neutered cats that I could name became alert, charming, active, delightful, and affectionate companions.

Dr. Johnson (and most other veterinarians) advises having cats, either male or female, altered * before they are six months old. The ideal age is between four and five months, depending on the size of the cat. The operation is not considered dangerous nowadays to either male or female cat; it is more difficult to perform on females—it is a major operation in which the ovaries and uterus are removed—but very few cats die.

With female cats the problem is not smell, but noise. As I've said before, some she-cats come in heat only once a year, some every two or three months, and some every four weeks. The every-four-week ones are the problem cats, of course.

* It is considered more genteel to speak of "altering" a cat of either sex than to use "spay" or "castrate" or "geld" to describe the operation.

The antics of a cat in heat are so extraordinary that people sometimes send for the vet and feel embarrassed when he tells them the facts of life. A she-cat in heat goes around in a peculiar crouch, forelegs down and hindlegs elevated, uttering anguished cries with a yelp at the end. Sometimes she eats, sometimes she doesn't. Sometimes she is extra affectionate, sometimes she ignores people. She always caterwauls. If there's a tomcat within miles, he shows up and caterwauls too. His caterwaul is different; it's a cat-size lion's roar. This goes on for three or four days.

One solution to this problem is kittens; there's quiet between caterwauling and kittens. There's also a brand-new problem— how to get rid of all those kittens? The other solution is to have the cat spayed. There is also the halfway measure of sterilization (an operation seldom performed, I am told) if you let the cat out and just don't want to bother with kittens. Otherwise it is useless because sterilization does not affect the cat's periods of heat, so she'll make all that fuss and not have any kittens to comfort her in her old age.

Some people give cats in heat dope to quiet them. They kill cats that way.

And, anyway, kittens are fun. They're uproarious, they're delightful, they're wonderful. Raising kittens keeps people young, it restores lost youth, it gives work for idle hands. I wish I had a litter of kittens scampering over the typewriter right now— there's no better excuse to stop working.

XII

Crime and Punishment

Cats respect and obey laws which make sense to them. Cats have no regard for red tape and niggling restrictions.

A cat makes up its mind what it wants and goes straight at it. If that try fails, the cat settles down and waits its chance and tries again. This single-mindedness is abhorrent to people who aren't happy unless they're bossing somebody around. With the peculiar, inverted reasoning which distinguishes tyrants, they say cats are sly. Sly! Cats are the most direct, forthright creatures I have ever known in my life. That's why crime is incomprehensible to them and punishment almost futile.

Palm-of-the-hand-to-seat-of-kitten-britches punishment does not seem to deter cats from any misdeeds. They are affronted, insulted, and willfully unrepentant. I have found that a rolled-up newspaper applied to the rear with loud bangs and little force does some slight good if not used too often. Once a cat finds out that you aren't going to kill it, nothing short of a deluge is convincing.

The most important single factor in punishing a cat is catching it in the act. If you come in and find milk spilled on the floor and the cat lapping it—that's the time for punishment. If you find milk all over the floor and the cat looking at it and not lapping, there's no mortal use in punishment, even though its whiskers are white with cream. The cat simply won't understand.

Scolding and nagging will accomplish nothing whatsoever. Beating or bullying will merely make the cat leave home. Cats refrain from sinning only when the game isn't worth the candle to them. There is no such thing as an obedient cat. When a cat does what it is asked to do, it obliges graciously.

MINE AND THINE

Cats' notions of mine and thine are quite unlike ours. They have a strong instinct for possession and not much sense of property. A cat with a mouse in its mouth is possession incarnate, but the mouse-hole is public domain. Cats do lay claim to hunting grounds and drive out invaders when game is scarce —if they didn't, they could not survive and stay free. They beat off strange cats and dogs that enter their gardens or their houses —this, I think, mainly because of sex jealousy and affection for their people, and partly because they like to be alone. Not that cats are hermits—they just don't like to be crowded. For example, a cat likes to have its own bed, and, after the gregariousness of kittenhood passes, doesn't want its litter brothers and sisters piling in. Pickle has a chateau, the lower shelf of a lamp table, on which he sits and meditates, and from which he ousts Ma and Charlie regularly. In short, cats are capitalists without the slightest wish for empire.

Cats take their food where they find it. They'll snatch food off anybody's plate, and if you can stop them you're good. I can't. In all my life I've known exactly two cats that didn't "steal" food, and I doubt if either of them would have stayed honest after missing a meal. I don't think cats regard taking food as stealing any more than Southern cooks look on toting as theft. A beanshooter used with relentless patience might persuade a cat to mend its taking ways.

CATS AND FURNITURE

Cats can learn to respect people's property. Or, rather, a cat that has its own soft cushion won't be so likely to covet your easy chair.

It is much more difficult to keep the cat from scratching your easy chair. Cats that live in the house must sharpen their claws in the house, and they quite reasonably prefer upholstered furniture to door-jambs and radiators. Direct punishment will do no good here because claw-sharpening *per se* isn't wrong and well the cat knows it. The only solution I ever found was to give the cat its own claw-sharpening place, such as a fireplace log with the bark on, a patented cat-scratching post, or an old rug. One of my friends, who found all of these lacking in claw-appeal, upholstered a log to match her living room sofa and her cats were delighted. If that fails, try some of the stuff that is supposed to keep cats off furniture and sometimes does.

Cats that go out are reasonable about furniture because they prefer real, live tree trunks. A whack or two with a rolled-up newspaper ought to deter any cat that can go out from insisting on an upholstered manicure.

You shouldn't cut a cat's claws, except when introducing it to a dog. Cutting them won't make the cat stop scratching furniture, it will only make Puss scratch harder to whittle the claws down to a point. Lack of claws may cause a cat to fall when otherwise it would have slipped and caught itself. I knew a cat that fell from a high window and was killed because its nails were clipped.

EXHIBITIONIST CATS

Exhibitionist cats are hard to manage. They don't bother anybody until company comes, and then, like undisciplined children, they show off all they know. It doesn't take a cat long to find out that crime has no consequences when there are guests about. If there's a cat hater among the guests, so much the better. It seems to me that Ma, Pickle, and Charlie must lie awake nights dreaming up ways to confirm cat haters in their bigotry. Whenever a cat hater visits us, they jump on tables, steal food, twine around my legs and trip me, miaou, whine, and spat with each other. Worst of all, they make violent love to the cat hater. Most of the cat haters I know are moderate cases, not quite ready for the booby hatch, and all they ask of my cats is to be let alone. Instead, they are walked on, kissed, pawed, scratched just enough to start runs in the stockings, and covered with cat hairs. The only cure I know is to put the cats out.

Some cats persecute cat haters by staring at them by the hour, unwinking and deliberate as if the cat hater were a mouse hole—it scares ailurophobes stiff. Other cats actually stalk cat haters. Whenever I see this I remember the oriental belief that people who hate cats were rats in another incarnation.

People who hate cats were rats in another incarnation

One cat I know plays with electric cords whenever there are guests, although he learned long ago that they were forbidden. Another pulls books off the shelves. Pickle used to go in and out the door, as often as anyone would open it for him, until I decided that out was enough. After that he did other things, all based on the simple premise that it's better to be spanked than ignored.

MICE AND SIN

From our point of view the worst crime cats commit is to torture the creatures they catch. From the cat's point of view, playing with a mouse is normal behavior, as normal as bull fighting to a Spaniard. Kittens in the cradle learn to hunt by catching the mice their mammas bring home and cripple slightly to make kitten toys. We can scarcely expect cats, who do us a great service when they catch vermin, to know their method of killing is wrong. By punishing a cat for playing with mice you can make it stop mousing; but that isn't the purpose. Whenever my cats used to bring in a mouse or rat alive, I hit it on the head with a hammer, shuddered, dropped it into the garbage can and praised the cat. To make sure of being understood I fed the cat something it particularly liked. As a result, my cats learned to kill their prey decently and quickly.

CATS AND OUR FEATHERED FRIENDS

Farm cats the world over know that chickens are not for them. The stupidest house cat can learn to respect the canary. Cats even learn to distinguish between wild and tame birds of the same species; I knew one cat that feasted on starlings in the barn and ate from the same dish with the starling that lived in her house. A cat can learn that it must not catch any birds in the house, that it must not catch any birds in the chicken yard, or that it must not catch any birds at all. I do not believe it would be possible to teach a cat that sparrows and starlings might be eaten, while robins and wrens were tabu. Such a rule wouldn't make sense to a cat. A cat is not capable of deciding between good and bad birds, moral and immoral birds. A cat learns that catching birds in a special place, or birds in general, is more trouble than it is worth, and for that reason lets birds alone.

Cats that grow up with poultry rarely think of them as food, and any erring kitten that starts dreaming of chicken dinner on the hoof gets a sound thrashing from the hen.

Cats that grow up with house birds may need a lesson or two. Cats that are suddenly introduced to house birds are pretty sure to need a lesson.

There are several ways of applying the lesson. A water pistol or a bean-shooter (neither of which can harm a cat) is a good tool. You pretend indifference until the cat crouches to spring. Then let go with beans or water. Don't scold the cat or shoo it; you want the cat to think the bird did that. If the cat knows you did, it will merely wait until you leave the room and then catch the bird. Righteous wrath is wasted—no cat will ever believe it's morally wrong to eat a canary. If the cat again shows interest in the canary, you repeat. Keep repeating until the cat gives up. The same system will work outdoors, but more vigilance is needed—much more.

When first we moved to the country Charlie caught an oriole and proudly brought it in, while we were entertaining a cat-hating caller, of course! I thrashed Charlie with the dead bird, and left it on the floor. Every time he stepped in the house we pointed out the dead oriole and scolded him, until he wouldn't

come in any more. I left the dead bird there until it stank.
Charlie never caught another bird. Indeed, he looked the other
way when he saw a bird.

Cats don't catch nearly as many birds as people think. A
healthy bird is not a pushover for any cat. After all, cats can't
fly and they are not especially brilliant tree climbers. One squirrel destroys more birds' eggs and baby birds in a year than a
score of cats. The birds cats catch are mainly sick birds or birds
beaten down by storms. After one heavy snowfall I dug more
than seventy birds out of the snow in an area of less than a
quarter of an acre. The body heat of the birds had melted the
snow so that they were entombed in small deep holes they
couldn't possibly get out of, which made them, literally, wind-
falls for any passing cat, dog, mink, weasel, or other bird-eating
animal. Heavy rains also beat birds to the ground. Extreme cold
numbs them and they fall. Migrating birds drop exhausted.
Sick birds go down to the ground to die. These are the birds
cats eat.

A cat that lives by hunting catches what comes easiest to
mouth, and, of all the creatures cats eat, birds are the very
hardest to catch. Ma, who used to be a wild cat, has never
shown any predatory interest in birds, while Pickle, who left
the woods before his eyes were open, had to be taught that birds
were forbidden, and Ben, his brother, never has been taught,
and he catches birds when he can.

If the cat does catch a bird, don't get too excited about it.
You eat birds, don't you? Consider that we, who could live
on vegetables, which cats cannot do, breed birds and rear them
tenderly so we may eat them. We hunt little birds. This is
called sport because it is unnecessary. I can see nothing sporting
in a man with dog and gun stalking a barnyard-reared pheasant.
Hunting, they say, is supposed to keep the pioneer spirit alive

Slatterns of the bird world

and to foster an interest in the conservation of nature's beauties. It also keeps the munitions makers busy between wars.

Then you might reflect on the fate of the passenger pigeon and the Carolina parakeet. Cats didn't exterminate them—people did it with guns and clubs and traps and their bare hands. Cats never have exterminated any creature. Once I met a woman who talked my ear off about the cruelty of cats to our feathered friends, and wound up by giving me a recipe for Robin Pie. I didn't believe people ate Robin Pie, so I looked it up and found that robins were popular food along the eastern seaboard as late as 1910, and that is why robins are scarce in our gardens.

On the other hand, Egypt, where cats were worshiped for centuries and are revered to this day, is a paradise for birds. The city of Jacksonville, Florida, is a bird sanctuary, the whole city, and I never have seen as many birds in my life as there are in Jacksonville. There are also a great many cats in Jacksonville, so it is plain that birds and cats can live together. In other parts of the country songbirds are scarce because people have killed them, destroyed their homes, and ruined their food supply. We have cut down the forests, drained the marshes, flooded the ponds with kerosene and sprayed them with DDT. Our native songbirds are mainly insectivorous—they can no more live on crumbs than cats can live on porridge—and when we poison the insects we bring famine to the birds. Also, because they are insectivorous, our songbirds need plenty of space for hunting. They can't and won't endure the slum conditions in which rats and people thrive. Only pigeons and starlings and sparrows, the slatterns of the bird world, will put up with us. All in all, virtuous indignation about a cat with a bird in its mouth ill becomes the best of us.

XIII

How Smart Is a Cat?

No human knows for certain what goes on in a cat's mind. We can only observe and interpret within the limits of our understanding, handicapped by the fact that we are people and cats are cats and the gap between us is as wide as creation.

We, in our simian way, insist on knowing a little about everything. We nibble every apple on the Tree of Knowledge in an endless search for perfection, which ends in rotten apples. Cats don't do that—to a cat, mice suffice.

Also, we brag. We stand upright—how long did it take you to learn, little man, and how often do you fall? We invented reading—and we read Dick Tracy; writing—half of us can't read our own scrawl; and arithmetic—there we have something, yet a cat can tell if a kitten is missing. We build towers into the sky—the better to bomb, my dear. We bounce echoes off the moon—and complain of the noise next door. We spend our lives building, making, inventing—and destroying. We split the atom, glimpsing God's miracle of creation—and we make it a weapon of war. We're the smartest creatures on earth.

We're smart, all right; but we're not the only wonderful beings. Can you jump ten times your height, walk a back fence with nonchalance, find your way swiftly through the dark, or catch a mouse with your teeth? Well, then, don't look down on cats. Cats don't gang up and try to exterminate each other. Cats don't wish to conquer the world—though, as Clarence Day pointed out, this might be a better world if cats ran it. At least cats know what they want.

Before we can attempt to judge how smart a cat is, we must find out what the cat can perceive because most thinking, human or animal, is based on sensory perception. Cats may know more about some things, including us, than we do, for their sensory organs are much more acute than ours.

THE SENSES

SIGHT

Cats see better than we do in dim light, and they see all right in broad daylight. Cats cannot see in total darkness.

I have watched Pickle jump ten feet across a dark floor, seemingly at nothing. When I went over, stooped and squinted, I found he had caught a silverfish, one of those tiny little bugs that live in books and old houses. I couldn't possibly see a silverfish at that distance.

Pickle chases butterflies in the summertime and his aim is perfect in the brightest sunlight.

When we lived in a fifth-floor apartment, Ma and Pickle used to sit on the windowsill and watch for me to come home. As soon as I turned the corner they'd stand up and rub against each other and pace back and forth, waving their tails, and when I reached the apartment door they'd be there waiting. Many times I slipped into the drug store on the corner and watched them dozing on the windowsill in the contented way of cats, seemingly oblivious to the bustle of the street. Then, the moment I stepped out the door, they'd be up and tail-waving. Recognizing a person five stories down and some three hundred feet away isn't a visual achievement for a person, of course; but it isn't bad seeing either.

Cats' eyes age, apparently, as ours do, for the Missus has grown farsighted lately, like a middle-aged person. She pushes any strange object away with her paw, tips her head back and squints down her nose like a dowager reading the menu at the Colony. If I drop a bite of food under her nose she doesn't even know it unless it has an odor. If it smells she snubbers blindly until she finds it. Toss a bite four or five feet ahead of her and she pounces on it.

Pickle and Charlie see well both near and far, though Pickle has a sharper eye for tiny things. Both of them seem to see best about a cat's jump ahead, which is probably what the Lord intended.

Color perception. Until about a year ago scientists were of the opinion that cats and all other mammals below the status of monkey were color-blind. That made no sense to me and I said so, loudly if unscientifically. You can imagine how I cheered when it was announced that experiments at the University of Chicago, under the direction of Dr. N. R. Brewer, have established that cats can distinguish colors. The cats are taught that if they push the red button they will be fed. After learning to do this, the cats unerringly select the red button in a row of buttons of many colors. The scientists still think dogs are color-blind.

Dozens of stories have come to me about cats that would sleep only on yellow cushions or eat from purple bowls or play with green balls or the like. I have observed absolutely nothing to confirm these stories. Some cats may be neurotic about the color of their cushions or their toys, but I'd have to see it.

Also, while it is established that cats can distinguish one color from another, I do not think they enjoy the contemplation of color as some of us do. When a cat sits facing the sundown with its paws tucked in and its eyes half shut, it is enjoying the warmth on its fur and the rich smell of afternoon, and doesn't care a hoot if the clouds are pea-green—it can't eat clouds.

Ma through the looking glass. There is a widespread belief that cats can't see themselves in mirrors. I accepted this unquestioningly until we moved into an apartment with a full-length mirror. During her first inspection tour Ma saw the cat in the glass, bristled, hunched, spat and attacked. Plainly she couldn't believe that paunchy, battle-scarred old trollop was herself.

After that she policed the mirror. She'd lie in ambush all day, waiting for the cat to come out and fight. At night she slept in a corner to protect her back and sides from assault. She tried to make Pickle fight the cat in the glass, which bewildered and dismayed him because Pickle couldn't see the cat.

Then one day the dogs upstairs had a fight. Ma heard it and ran to the mirror. The dog fight upstairs wasn't a patch on Ma's mirror fight. Finally exhaustion slowed her down, bruised and bloody, but unbowed. She backed away and studied her adversary. The cat in the glass looked just as bad. She backed again, to a safe distance, sat down and licked her bleeding paws, wiped her battered face, glancing anxiously at the glass every few seconds. The glances became long looks. She got up and advanced cautiously, her hackles wavering up and down. She studied the cat in the glass dubiously. She licked a paw and wiped her face, still watching the cat. Then she wiped the glass. Then she licked the glass. She sat back and meditated.

After a long time she went and got Pickle, led him to the mirror. She looked at Pickle and looked at his reflection. She studied him full face and in profile. Watching herself closely, she licked Pickle's ear and patted the glass as if to show him his reflection.

After a while Pickle saw himself. He gaped at his image and gawked at Ma. They spent the rest of the day studying themselves and their reflections.

In time they learned to use the mirror, as women in Holland use *spionnetjes* (little mirrors set cater-cornered to the windows so they can watch the neighbors without being seen). Ma and Pickle would sit four or five feet in front of the mirror and to one side, where they could see the whole room and every movement people made. They evolved a ball game that consisted in batting the ball away from the mirror, then whirling to look in the glass and see where it went. This has remained their favorite game and they taught it to Charlie. Pickle never tires of the wonder of having eyes in the back of his head.

I think if a mirror is placed in a good light, exactly vertical, and comes down to the floor, most cats can see themselves. Some cats, like some people, have defective vision.

I have not succeeded in making pictures recognizable to a cat. This is a disappointment because I used to know a parakeet that looked at bird pictures as eagerly as a child and whooped with glee when he came to his kind of bird. Perhaps my cat pictures aren't as clear as those bird prints were.

A few years ago someone gave me a plaster cat, a copy of the Hidari Jingora statue which has been kept by silkworm breeders

in Japan since the Sixteenth Century to scare rats away. I set
the plaster cat, which was about the size of Charlie and painted
black, on the stairs leading to the garden and waited to see what
would happen. The cats discovered it simultaneously, when they
came in to supper. They growled and ganged up on it. The
cat didn't move and one of those long silences followed. Charlie
broke it by jumping on the cat, which went over with a lifeless
thud. A plaster ear chipped off. Ma and Pickle gave Charlie
one long, cold look and stalked past the broken statue into the
house. Charlie followed them sheepishly.

HEARING

Cats hear the wee patter of mice, the slither of snakes and a
thousand small brustling rustles that we couldn't hear to save us.

Cats also hear the rumble of traffic, the bang of hammers
and the roar of machines; they hear the strange whining we
call music and the endless clack of human talk. Cats filter these
sounds in some manner known only to themselves, and disre-
gard all noises which don't concern them. This is an art. Think
what a lovely world this would be if people refused to hear anything that was none of their business.

Because cats won't clutter their heads with our racket, a few
misguided souls think they are tone-deaf. Except blue-eyed
white cats—which, as I said before, are nearly always born completely deaf—cats hear a lot better than we do. Their tonal
range is wider than ours, and their ears are sharper. The fact that
cats do not care for what western Europeans are pleased to call
music is a matter of taste, and one which they share with the
overwhelming majority of the human race. Only the cantankerous tribes of western Europe and their descendants find melody
in combinations of full and half tones in the middle range of
sound. Other peoples have more subtle ideas. The rest of the

world (including the Chinese and the Scots) finds half tones, quarter tones, eighth tones, sixteenth tones, and even thirty-second tones, pleasing to the ear, as cats do. This doesn't mean they're deaf, it means they're different.

Pickle and Charlie used to recognize the footsteps of their friends five flights down in the noisy city and went to the door to meet them before I knew anyone was coming.

A slam of the refrigerator door calls Pickle and Charlie from the ends of the block. I often slam it to call them at suppertime. I have tried slamming other doors to see if they would answer, and they didn't.

They can be fooled, though. The first time Charlie heard a bird in the radio he nearly lost his wits. And one year, before Charlie, a mocking bird lived in our garden. In no time it learned to imitate my toneless whistle which called the cats. It lured the cats away from home. It called them home when they weren't wanted. When I did want them that confounded bird whistled first from one place and then another, until the cats and I were hopelessly provoked.

About the time I found Charlie, Ma retired. She took to dozing beside the fire, and if Pickle went off to investigate a mouse hole she'd nudge Charlie into following him. This disgusted Pickle, who didn't want a flighty kitten galloping around his mouse holes. It puzzled me until I realized that Ma was growing deaf. She's deaf as a post now, but, like most deaf people, tries to pretend she isn't. If she's asleep at suppertime, I have to shout in her ear to wake her. She unfailingly blinks, shakes herself and gives me a dirty look, much as to say, "You don't have to yell like that—I heard you the first time."

Cats' reliance on their ears got a lot of them in trouble during the early days of the war. Since cats began to sail the seas they had assumed the right to go ashore in every port, depending

on the ship's whistles to call them back at sailing time. The half
hour whistle called the crew aboard. The fifteen minute whistle
summoned stragglers. The final toot, five minutes before cast-
ing off, was the cat's whistle. Then war silenced the whistles
and cats that depended on their ears were marooned in every
port. In March, 1942, the New York papers printed photographs of a sea cat named Minnie whose paw was sought by
the masters of sixteen United Nations ships, their own cats
having been beached in other silent ports. I heard of one cat
stranded in Panama for months, who lived on the docks, waiting for her ship. She refused dozens of seductive offers to sail
with other vessels, and when her own ship did come in she
was first aboard with four fat kittens. Some cats still wait for
whistles that never will blow again.

SMELL

The pleasures of smelling. Of all mammals, only men, monkeys, and cats show esthetic delight in pleasant smells. Cats are
more civilized in their enjoyment of perfume than we are. In
our shiftless way we use pleasant scents to cover up unpleasant ones, and all too seldom smell for smelling's sake. We excuse ourselves by saying our olfactory nerves are degenerate,
which they certainly are. We ruined them with smoke, soot, coal
gas, hot food, alcohol, unsanitary housing, and other comforts
of civilization. If we could smell as well as cats we probably
wouldn't be able to stand ourselves. Some of the "clean" chemical odors with which we try to disguise our smells are utterly
revolting to cats; but with admirable patience they try to ignore
our stinks and make the most of any sweet-scentedness that
comes their way.

Pickle and Ben were kittens in the country in the summertime, and each morning and evening they went all around the

Smelling like a femme fatale

garden smelling. When he came to the sweet alyssum Pickle dropped flat on his belly and smelled himself dizzy. Ben preferred roses, with petunias for second choice. They played a game with petunias and ragged robins, tapping the blossoms back and forth without ever breaking one. I never knew either of them to destroy a flower intentionally. Once in a while Charlie swipes a flower from a vase and takes it to bed with him.

Ma likes strong-scented flowers, which may be because she's old and her senses are beginning to fail.

She does love a real loud smell. Once I bought some bad flea powder that burned her, and after the first application she ran and hid as soon as the can appeared. I got good flea powder and she wouldn't have it either. She was tormented by fleas and something had to be done, so I bought a box of highly perfumed face powder, awful, smelly stuff, and mixed a little with the good flea powder, then spilled some as if by accident. Ma sniffed, purred and rolled in it. I shook a dash in my hand and rubbed her face with it. She was delighted, and for the rest of the flea season the Missus went around smelling like a *femme fatale,* and mighty proud of herself she was.

One of my friends who has been plagued for years by admiring felines recently learned that the perfume she used had a base of wild thyme blossoms, which made her slightly catnipaceous.

Catnip is the ultimate in smell appreciation. We have nothing to compare with it. Catnip ecstasy is above and beyond any sensual pleasure people have discovered since they started keeping records. You've only to see the contempt of a cat for a drunk to realize it. Catnip intoxicates without drunkenness. It is absinthe without regret, champagne without consequences. Under the influence of catnip young cats grow bold and old cats find their youth again. I imagine the ancient Greeks, who loved cats, must have envisioned the Elysian Fields as eternal catnip-beds, as cats would if they dreamed of immortality.

The practical use of smell. Smelling isn't all catnip and cologne. Cats sniff out occupied mouse-holes and snake-holes, detect approaching enemies, locate well-stocked kitchens and form opinions of people.

When cat haters and people with scary little dogs come to visit, I put the cats out. It is amusing to watch them, after the guests have gone, inspecting their house inch by inch, following the trail from door to chair. Their whiskers twitch and feel; their hackles bristle, waver or lie serenely flat as they find the departed visitor hateful, dubious, or likeable.

At first meeting with a stranger they stand off and sniff; then make friends or not as their noses dictate. Since they don't sniff loudly or obviously, the strangers seldom realize they're being smelled. I think cats judge people largely by smell, because I can't account for their fancies otherwise. They've made friends with people who vowed they hated cats, with people who stead-fastly ignored them until all three piled in their laps, and even with people who gushed and burbled at them. And then again they've refused to go near nice people who seemed genuinely fond of them. This, I think, explains why some people who like cats aren't able to make friends with them. Cats won't love you unless you smell good to them.

TASTE

Taste is closely related to smell, and here too cats are civi-lized.

We all admit that cats are epicures because they're fond of chicken and cream and other rich, expensive delicacies which we like too. Some cats prefer dainties to coarse food, though the

coarse food is better for them, and this evidence of refinement
tempts people to overfeed them. Other cats like hearty fare,
and they are gourmets too. Ma will eat anything that contains garlic, whether it is cat food or not. Pickle is a connoisseur
of ripe old Cheddar cheese. Charlie, the unfillable, detests garlic and cheese but will sell his soul for a chicken head. All the
cats I've ever known were choosey about their food. And for
all we know, mice are delectable—the Indians ate them, and
I've just learned that in the neighborhood of Genoa, Italy,
Mouse Pie is a popular delicacy.

TOUCH

We have only a foggy notion of the things cats perceive
through their whiskers, their paws and their fur.

Whiskers. Cats' whiskers serve as feelers to determine the
character of strange objects, and, to a limited degree, as calipers.
It is not true that cats' whiskers span the exact breadth of the
cat and are used to gauge just what a cat can get into and out
of successfully. If that were so, cats wouldn't be forever getting
stuck in chimneys, holes, and drain pipes. Some cats have stubby
little whiskers not nearly as wide as themselves, and they may
be the ones that get stuck, though I'm inclined to believe that
stupid cats get stuck and bright cats do not. Some male cats
have positively ornamental whiskers which they care for so
lovingly that only vanity explains them. Kittens, who are full of
the spirit of adventure and short on judgment, have the merest
beginning of whiskers, though they'd need them more than
sedate old cats if whiskers were measuring rods.

Whiskers are used as feelers by adult cats. Whenever a cat
investigates a strange object it sniffs and then the whisker-tips
move forward and explore the surface, stroking it all over deli-
cately and thoroughly. In some fashion which people don't

understand, a cat learns more this way than eyes, ears, and nose can tell it. I think some of us (though not all) distinctly approach this form of perception through our hands. We know more about any wonderful thing, whether an apple, a jewel, a book or a baby, after we have held it and felt of it all over—we know whether it is good or bad, genuine or shoddy, and have no idea how we know, it just "feels" right, or wrong. Cats' whiskers tell them a great deal more than this, either through their own sensitivity or by sharpening the other faculties.

The notion that cats have learned to use their whiskers as compensation for poor sight was thought up and passed on by small-minded souls who didn't believe a cat could have anything we haven't got. This idea of a cat myopically tapping its whiskers ahead of it like a blind man with a cane is absurd to anyone who has ever observed the speed and grace of a cat in motion. If a cat got caught out in utter darkness it might use its whiskers to help find the way home, though it would be far likelier to curl up right there and sleep until daybreak.

Just as an inquisitive cat extends its whiskers to investigate, so a happy cat lays them back and smooths them back and takes great pleasure in it. Cats show affection for each other by rubbing faces, nose tips to ears, stroking their whiskers with each movement. Cats rub their bodies against any friendly person who might have food or warmth to spare. They stroke their whiskers only against people they really love. Charlie rubs cheeks, as if I were another cat. Ma and Pickle like to push their noses hard into the palm of a hand and then stroke the whiskers back.

Whisker perception does not seem to diminish with age. Now that her other senses have begun to fail, Ma pats with her paw and feels with her whiskers before accepting any strange object as harmless.

Paws. Cats use their paws cleverly and sensitively. When Charlie was little he always put a paw in his food and licked it clean before eating, and still does if his dinner is the least bit warmer than it should be. Sometimes he sits up like a squirrel, holding a bite in his paws, and eats it that way. When he feels affectionate he pats my face with his paws, between whisker swipes, and plainly likes the feel of it, as I enjoy stroking his fur.

When Ma had kittens she was wonderfully dexterous in moving the least one up to the milk supply and holding Ben and Pickle off when they'd had enough. She can open any door or drawer that is not too heavy.

Then of course all cats knead their friends with their paws, and the happier they are the more industriously they knead. This seems to be a habit formed when they are nursing kittens and instinctively knead their mammas' teats to make the milk flow faster; later, it expresses contentment without milk.

The delight cats take in feeling any pleasant surface is proverbial. A bearskin before the cave man's fire may have been almost as great an inducement as mice when cats took up with him. This is a basic part of being cats, and extends to the care they take of their own smooth coats.

Fur. We know cat fur is electric, that it crackles when brushed in cold weather and actually shows faint sparks when rubbed briskly in the dark. Not knowing the cause or purpose of this, we ignore it, and go right on saying that cats are psychic or that they have a sixth sense. Perhaps some cats are psychic (I once owned a dog that saw ghosts), but isn't it simpler to suppose that having bodies covered with highly electric fur makes cats extra sensitive to approaching changes of weather, or even other disasters? Our own hair is somewhat electrified and if brushed vigorously in cold, dry weather may spark a trifle. It becomes limp before or during a rainy spell, and stiffens up when the sun is about to shine. A lot of people (I, for one) have been frightened or angry enough to feel a prickling of the scalp and an actual bristling at the nape of the neck. I also feel this when a thunder storm approaches. Suppose we were covered all over with electrically-charged hair—we could fire the weather man.

REASON

In order to stay free and survive, cats exercise the faculty of reason. By making intelligent use of their powers of perception they deduce inferences from premises much as we do when we learn the hard way—by experience. Cats learn everything the hard way. Their schooling ends when mamma's milk dries up, and after that they're on their own, with observation to take the place of books, and experience for a teacher.

Theory has no place in a cat's life, as it has in ours. When we discover, for example, that what goes up must come down, a fact well known to any cat that ever climbed a tree, we can't possibly let it go at that. We must know why things fall, how fast they fall, where they'll land and how hard they'll hit. We invest each discovery with that magical quality called Reason, and assure ourselves for the squindillionth time that we alone in all this world are endowed with it. By means of mathematics, calculus, and theorematic diagrams we reduce the whole thing to abstraction, and teach our children the Theory of a Tumble. But do we tell them not to sit under an apple tree? No indeed. By the time we start teaching we've forgotten what it feels like to be bopped by a pippin. Consequently a lot of pupils leave school thinking Isaac Newton discovered the Law of Gravity while selling apples on a street corner, and don't find out the truth until an apple or a depression falls on them. A cat up a tree is different.

Once Ma, Pickle, and I lived in a grove of pine trees that shot up thirty, forty feet and more, culminating in scraggy dusters of twigs and needles. Ma and Pickle were fascinated by those trees, and in time Pickle climbed one and considered himself stuck. I tried to get him down and couldn't. The neighbors tried and they couldn't. The local fire department wasn't interested. Night came and Pickle still teetered on a flimsy little branch, silhouetted against the moon like a witch's cat, mewing and moaning. Finally in despair I climbed on the car and poked him off with a long pole. The ground was soft and it didn't hurt him. Like Mark Twain's cat that jumped on the hot stove, Pickle kept out of all trees after that.

Then Ma got stuck. She shinned up the tallest tree, where I couldn't reach her even with a pole, so I sat down at the foot of the tree with a dish of meat and called her. She moaned and cursed and squalled, and then sat still and meditated, or whatever cats do when they sit still. After a long time she clutched the trunk with her forepaws, swung her hind legs part way round the tree and gripped with them. Next she swung the front of her sidewise and slightly downward. Loose bark shattered and I thought every moment she would fall. She worked her way down in a slow precarious spiral, slipping and clawing and grunting, until she was low enough to jump. I hugged her and said, "Now, you old fool, you'll have sense enough to keep out of trees." You think so? Not the Missus. Having reasoned out the problem of descent, she went up every tree on the place for the fun of coming down again.

Every cat that has the opportunity catches one toad. No cat in its right mind catches a second toad. Pickle caught his toad and was thoroughly burned by the scalding exudation that is a toad's only defense. Pickle wallowed in self pity for a day or so, and after his mouth healed he still cringed at sight of a toad. He also avoided frogs, though Ma was feasting high on them. When Ma caught a frog he'd run and try to slap her away from it. When that failed, he'd sit back in anxious bewilderment and watch her eat it. She'd guzzle and smack her chops, showing that frogs were good. She ignored toads.

Pickle followed her about for days, watching and plainly worrying. Then one evening I saw the Missus sitting contentedly on the stoop beside a big fat mammy toad that was catching moths as they fluttered against the screen. Pickle was pacing back and forth in the garden, mewing fearfully. I sat down on the stoop and stroked the mammy toad's back while she ate a large gray moth, rolling her eyes to push it along. Pickle fidgeted and peeped and clawed at my skirt. The next evening Ma and the toad were on the stoop again. Pickle crouched at the edge, fascinated and ready to run. The third evening they all sat together. Every evening afterward, until frost put an end to moths and sent the mammy toad underground for her winter's sleep, Ma and Pickle and the toad communed. In time Pickle learned that frogs were different and good to eat.

The stages of Pickle's reasoning were clear. Starting with the premise that if it moves it's food, he caught a toad. The toad burned his mouth, showing that the initial premise was partially incorrect. This led him to conclude that all hopping things were dangerous. He persisted in this belief until Ma demonstrated that frogs were good to eat and even toads were harmless unless bitten. Finally, he learned to distinguish between frogs and toads. That was all he needed to know about batrachians.

Ma believes that what is good for people is good for cats, and sometimes she's right. Once the Missus and I had a cold together. Our eyes ran, our noses ran, and she drooled. When she climbed in my lap for sympathy she dripped on me, so I wiped her nose with a paper handkerchief. After that when her nose ran she went to the paper handkerchief box, hooked out a paw-ful, dragged them to me wherever I was, and held her face up.

The Missus isn't above a spot of skulduggery in a good cause, either. When she came to me out of the woods I lived with a macaw, an old little blind canary and a field mouse named Daisy. Within half an hour Ma caught Daisy. I rescued Daisy unhurt, carried her out in the back yard and explained that field mice lived in fields, come spring, and turned her loose. I didn't see Daisy again. Field mice are nice.

The macaw, I reckoned, could look out for himself. Mac did. He watched Ma silently until she noticed him. While she was still gawking, Mac spread his scarlet wings full width, twisted his head upside down, and said, "Hello. Carajo. Scat!" Ma jumped almost out of her skin, and Mac was safe after that. He teased Ma unmercifully and had a wonderful time playing with the kittens.

Ma didn't seem to notice the canary for several days, until she asked for food between meals—she was so starved I fed her every time I looked at her, but this time I said she'd have to wait. She yelled at me and I told her to hush her fuss. She said, "Now!" furiously, stalked into the dining room, sat down under the canary's cage and glowered up at it. I fed her quick. The next time she got hungry she asked for food, demanded it, and threatened the canary again. It was the rankest blackmail I ever saw. As the kittens grew up she taught them to threaten the canary. But when Ben got an enterprising notion about eating the canary, Ma spanked him hard. That canary was worth more to her than the goose that laid the golden eggs, and she men-aced him tenderly until he died of old age. Ma's reasoning needs no explanation. Her ability to figure out a blackmail plot leaves me in bewildered chuckles every time I recall the Missus and her four fat kittens lined up under the canary cage.

Ben Britton is Ma's son and he's as smart as the Missus, which —possibly excepting Charlie's pixie brilliance—is about as smart as a cat can be. Last summer Ben's folks went away for a week-end and asked me to feed him. They didn't want to leave doors or windows standing open while they were gone, so they asked me to keep Ben indoors. I tried—nobody can keep Ben in when he wants out. He sailed across the garden and over the fence and away. At suppertime I whistled, and Ben came sauntering along the fence, peering through the fantastic wire maze that was supposed to "cat proof" his garden, telling me he couldn't get in. I knew he could, but I didn't know how. I climbed on a chair, held my arms up and told him to jump. Ben considered that a long time, shook his tail, and went down into the next yard and scratched at the gate. I let him in and thought no more about it until his folks came home. I told them Ben got out and, merely to make conversation, described his home coming. They were amazed. In all of his seven years Ben had come through one gap in the maze and had not returned to his garden in any other way. Whenever possible he had induced someone to stand under the gap and catch him when he jumped. I'd offered to catch him, but had stood in the wrong place, so Ben made it easy for me.

One morning when Ben went out for his daily stroll, a little dog rushed out of the house next door, barking wildly, and chased Ben up onto the fence. Ben sat on the fence and pon-dered, ashamed probably and certainly puzzled. Ben liked dogs. He lived with a dog half as big and twice as yappy as the cocker that was calling him such awful names. Finally Ben went home. The next day the cocker chased him again, and the next and the next and the next. Then one night Ben went into the little dog's house, found it asleep in its beribboned basket, and beat it up. He didn't exactly fight the cocker and didn't injure it, just thrashed it. After that one punitive expedition Ben walked through the cocker's yard every day, slowly, and the cocker didn't bark. In time they were seen sunning themselves side by side. If human reasoning had more of Ben's simplicity and human behavior its directness, this might be a less complicated world.

Cats can plan ahead to an amazing degree, if the end result is apt to benefit them. Charlie was a tiny little mite when I found him, still a toddler when he walked, though able to run like a blue streak until he struck some immovable object and was knocked sprawling. Ma and Pickle would have none of him—he'd eat up their food, he'd wiggle into my heart. They so persecuted him that I didn't dare leave Charlie alone with them. Pickle's hostility thawed gradually into huffiness. The Missus was adamantly murderous until one evening, when Charlie was four or five months old, she came into the kitchen while he was eating, bristled at sight of his chubby little back and started toward him, stiff-legged and ready to do battle. About halfway she paused; the bristles wavered. She stared at Charlie, tiptoed nearer, and inspected his rear-end thoroughly. She turned and gave me a filthy look, much as to say, "Why didn't you tell me this was a tomcat?" and began to wash his ear. From that moment on Charlie was her darling. Lovingly and tenderly she raised him to be her beau.

Cats vary in their ability to reason out a problem, as they vary in all things, and, since passing grade for a cat is bare survival, a lot of them get by without showing any great intellectual capacity. But any cat able to make its own way learns from experience and adapts established habits in order to cope with new situations. In order to keep the breed alive, cats transmit acquired knowledge to other cats—as mamma cats do when they bring educational mice to their kittens, and as Ma did when she showed Pickle the difference between frogs and toads. Cats adjust themselves to a changing world better than any other creatures; only cats can go wild and become tame again, equally at home in a hollow tree or a rocking chair. Cats achieve success, with us or without us, by the exercise of reason, however limited. Cat reasoning differs only in degree, and not at all in kind, from our thinking—the dissimilarity is in our point of view. And in the long run there isn't so much difference between a million dollars and a good mouse hole.

TALENTED CATS

Most cats have a talent of some sort if their people will take the pains to develop it. House cats are handy in all sorts of ways, some of them provoking. Ma used to open the refrigerator and help herself to whatever she fancied. When she taught Pickle to raid the ice box, I gave up and moved. They continued to try each new refrigerator, so now I rent apartments with high-handled refrigerators.

All three cats open doors that aren't securely latched. They always claw at the side that opens, even in a new apartment. Pickle has learned that when he can't open a door, persistent scratching and loud wails will fetch a person to open it for him. Charlie stretches up and paws at the knob, though he hasn't yet managed to open a door that is securely latched, thank goodness. Some cats really open doors. *Life* magazine recently printed a series of photographs showing a cat that jumped up, grasped the doorknob in her paws, turned it, dropped back and went in.

Once I accidentally shut Charlie in a closet. The house was

very old and the closet door was fastened by means of a wooden pin that bridged a gap between door and door-jamb. I was on my way to let Charlie out when I saw his paw—a couple of toes really—come through the crack, push the pin down, and out bounced Charles. That seemed too clever to be intentional, so a few days later I shut Charlie in the closet. He got out in less than two minutes. We made a game of it for a while, until Charlie became so skilled we both were bored.

When an animal learns that a straight line is not necessarily the shortest distance between two points, it really has achieved something. A day or two after moving into this house, I let the cats out in the back yard and, because the weather was nice, left them there. Ma and Pickle miaoued and scratched at the back door. Charlie vanished. A few minutes later he came swaggering down the street and scratched at the front door. The block is solidly lined with houses and at first I couldn't imagine how he went from gardens to street. Later I learned that he crossed two back yards, went into the cellar of the apartment house, followed an elaborate system of corridors and passageways to an upper hall, came down the front stairs and waited until someone opened the street door so he could come home. He had passed through his own front door only once, shut up in a carrier, and how he found it and recognized it is a mystery to me.

Pickle learned Charlie's route, of course, but he seldom goes on the street. Last time the Missus was in heat Charlie escorted her through the labyrinth and ensconced her on a front basement window sill. There she reclined, like the painting of Cleopatra on her barge, surrounded by eager swains, while Charlie tramped up and down in front of the house, piping tomcats from all over town, to the hilarious amusement of the neighbors.

Ben is an acrobat. For five long years his people tried by every means they could devise to cat-proof their back yard so as to keep Ben in and strange cats out. Rube Goldberg would admire the fixings on their fence. They finally succeeded in keeping strange cats out. They didn't even dishearten Ben. I have seen him go straight up that eight foot fence and, hanging upside down, work his way across a horizontal strip of chicken wire two feet wide, and swing up and over. I have also seen Ben climb five stories up a vertical fire ladder (not a stairway or a fire escape with landings—a ladder) to visit a friend who might have sardines in the pantry, and climb down again.

Then there was Henry the firehouse cat of West Forty-third Street, in New York, who brightened the lives of his brigade by sliding down the firemen's pole at the drop of a bite of liver, or just for fun, until on a summer day in 1942 Henry slid down the pole, meandered out into the sunshine and was seen no more.

Country cats have opportunities to develop special skills which are unknown to city cats. For one, country cats go fishing, while few city cats ever heard of the sport. The famous *Rue du Chat Qui Pêche,* in Paris, used to be literally the Street of the Fishing Cat when its cellars flooded every time the Seine was high; then the quay was built and the name of the tiny street became a quaint anachronism.

Country cats have a lot of fun fishing; some learn to dive for fish or water rats. Cats don't mind getting wet if it's to their advantage. Ma used to get her sea food the easy way. At the foot of our hill there was a swamp. The man who owned the swamp lived at the edge of it, in an amphibious shack with a canoe tied to the back porch, and hunted frogs for market. Soon Ma began coming home with frog bodies, which I supposed he'd thrown to her, because they weren't worth anything. Then she started fetching frogs' legs, neatly severed. Frogs' legs sold for $1.20 a pound. I visited the frog hunter and said I hoped my old cat didn't bother him. He said no indeed, he liked her, gave her all the "frawg-tops" she could eat and tote. I said, "I'm afraid she's been stealing frogs' legs from you." He thought that was funny—no cat could get his frogs' legs, they were "kivered up right good." For the rest of the frog season Ma brought home enough frogs' legs to feed us all, if I'd accepted her offers to share.

Most good cats are generous with their catches. One talented cat in Massachusetts used to bring home full-grown hens, squawking and uninjured, for the Sunday dinner, to the embarrassment of his folks and the indignation of the neighbors. Chicken stealing is reprehensible, of course, and not to be condoned, but the talented aren't always virtuous.

The two cats that follow rate as geniuses in my book, and certainly they are virtuous. The first is a white Persian cat named Baby that lives with Mrs. Carolyn Swanson at Hermosa Beach, California. Baby is a Seeing-Eye cat. When Mrs. Swanson became totally blind Baby undertook the job of guiding her, and within a year had mastered it. They go everyplace together, Baby on a lead, switching his tail against her legs at street-crossings, pulling ahead when the traffic stops, signaling steps up and down.

Impy is just as remarkable. Impy is a black cat of the sort called common. He is Hearing-Ear cat for Mrs. Violet Gooding, of Gooding, Idaho. Impy and his assistant "ear," a black dog named Inky, do all of Mrs. Gooding's hearing for her. They wake her when the alarm rings in the morning, lead her to the kitchen when a pot boils over; Impy taps Mrs. Gooding's foot when visitors knock at the door, and warns her of any strange sound.

TRICKS

Most cats consider tricks beneath their dignity. The few ex-
hibitionists that are willing to learn tricks simply adore them,
and will think up tricks for themselves if they live with un-
imaginative people.

Almost any cat will sit erect and catch bits of meat that are
thrown to it, though it wouldn't be diplomatic to call this "beg-
ging" within earshot of the cat. Most cats will roll over when
they are told to, if they know their tummies will be tickled each
time they roll. They do this because they roll when they're
happy and they like to be tickled. Other cats sit erect and box,
with their claws nicely turned in. These are all things that
cats teach themselves, with a little help from people, because
they like to do them.

Francie, a black and white cat I used to know, invented a
lovely trick. He performed only when guests were present,
preferably strangers, because the trick startled them, and Francie, short for François Villon, was scamp enough to enjoy that.
Francie would begin by stalking the woman he lived with,
switching his tail and growling. He'd keep that up until all
conversation ceased and the guests were watching him ap-
prehensively. Then his woman would raise her arm and he'd
spring, still growling like a tiger. He'd wrap all four legs around
her arm and hang there, roaring and rumbling and pretending
to chew her arm off, until she got tired and let him down. In
all the eight years of his life Francie never was known to scratch
anyone.

Beyond a feeble ambition to teach Charlie to walk a tightrope,
which glimmered out before he was old enough to learn, I never
tried to teach a cat tricks. A friend of mine who knows a very

great deal about cats and has taught them all sorts of things
contributed the following advice, which I know is good:

"First, a cat must be in the mood, must be pleased, must be
liking the teacher of the tricks that particular day and hour.

"Second, the cat should be no younger than three months, and
may be much older.

"Third, the cat cannot be punished for failure to do the trick
or failure to concentrate. It doesn't like doing tricks anyway, except in rare cases, and the learning and performance must be ac-
companied by praise, flattery, and immediate rewards.

"A meal during the day is the best time for learning, not in
the evening, for a cat may have other things on its mind at
night.

"Say the same thing over and over, as, 'Sit up!' Make the cat
do it, very gently, and give it a bit of its dinner. Repeat this for
five or ten minutes—not more—day after day, every day, until
that trick is an established habit and the cat will sit up without
wondering whether it wants to or not every time it hears the
words.

"You must be careful not to tire the cat by too long concentration, or it may grow to hate the tricks. If it is taught in the
atmosphere of sycophantic admiration that cats seem to like
it may even take a modest pride in its accomplishments. It
should always be rewarded, though, like a seal, if not with a tid-
bit of food, then with praise, chin scratching, patting.

"By this method a cat can be taught to sit up, lie down and
roll over, shake hands, jump through hands or a hoop, jump
from one chair to another, or about anything else that a cat is
able to do without discomfort."

My friend's old Persian cat learned so well that after eight
years of inattention, while its mistress was away at school and
college, growing up, it ran through its whole repertoire when

she went home for a visit. Later she had a wildcat that learned to fetch its ball and do a few other tricks.

CRAZY CATS

If proof were needed that cats can think, we'd have it in the fact that some cats can't.

I used to know a woman who lived with a whole pack of idiot cats, identical in beauty and brainlessness. They showed individuality only by finding different places to hide when visitors came, and from that glimmer their names derived. Boy hid on the highboy in the hall, Beddy under the bed, Kitchy in the kitchen, and so on.

Cats like that don't survive in alleys. In the cattery they are not uncommon. One of nature's nastier pranks is to produce, every now and then, a strain of animals so beautiful that the temptation to perpetuate them is almost irresistible, and so stupid that we know perfectly well we shouldn't permit them to reproduce.

Moronic cats are scarcer than idiot animals of other kinds, and if cat breeders would only make up their minds to breed for brains as well as beauty, pretty soon all pure-bred cats would be geniuses—and think how many more would be bought.

The most efficient little cat I ever lived with had an idiot kitten, so stupid it didn't know enough to come in out of the rain, too dumb to catch a mouse, even too dumb to play with the mice its mamma brought in. Although Phoebe wasn't deaf, she never learned to answer to her name. I think Kits knew Phoebe was an idiot, because she nursed the kitten and treated it like a baby until a dog killed feeble Phoebe when she was two years old.

Spattie was a borderline case. She was raised by a little lonely monkey who rocked her to sleep and fed her blackberries, which she hated, and fought everyone except me who touched the kitten. Spattie was the only cat I ever heard of that got bit by a fish. She liked to drink out of the aquarium, which was the home of a large pair of Acaras. The fish always had been there and I don't suppose Spattie ever thought of catching them. Spring came and the Acaras scooped out a nest in the sand, laid eggs, and tenderly cared for their babies. One day I heard an odd sound and found Spattie straddling the tank helplessly, while the male fish swung from the tip of her tongue, lashing furiously, and the female herded her babies to the farthest corner. Apparently it never occurred to Spattie that by pulling her tongue in she could get a nice five-dollar shore dinner.

I think the kindest thing to do with an idiot cat is to have it killed painlessly by the vet. People sometimes become attached to stupid cats and of course they should keep them— but I most emphatically think defective cats should be sterilized so they can't further demoralize their breed.

Insane cats are rare, but they do exist. Very occasionally a kitten is born crazy and stays that way. Insane cats are not necessarily, or even usually, stupid. They're just nuts. One of the most efficient ratters I ever knew was a big black tomcat that terrorized the whole block for several months. He was a fighting fool. He killed kittens. Any decent self-respecting cat that sat quietly on its own fence in the sun was likely to be attacked without warning. When he took to invading houses and attacking people, the S.P.C.A. was notified and he was taken away. I have known only two such cats in my life and have heard of another, which speaks very well for the sanity of cats. Those cats can't be cured, and I think they should be killed humanely.

On the other hand, sane cats can become insane, and they can be cured.

Pickle the dignified, His Pickleship the pompous, Monsieur du Piquel the pseudo-intellectual, was insane for one whole year. Until he was six months old Pickle was a normal, rambunctious kitten. Then I had him altered. The operation is so simple that butchers and barbers continued to perform it long after veterinarians had become fairly plentiful. Pickle was operated on by a skilled, gentle veterinarian, and yet he came home from the hospital a mental wreck.

For slightly more than a year he was afraid of everything and everybody. If he saw his shadow against the wall he'd run and hide. He was afraid of hands and faces, and he had a special horror of people's feet. He spent half of that year with his poor scared little face buried in Ma's fur to shut out this terrible world. He lived in an apartment, sheltered and loved, and he got no better. He was even afraid of me, and I had taken him out of the hollow tree before his eyes were open. If I hadn't been sentimental about the Missus and her woods kittens, I would have had him put out of his very real misery. Then, almost exactly a year after his "breakdown," I took the cats to the country.

Ma was delighted. She shinned up and down tree trunks, chased frogs, cavorted like a silly kitten. Pickle stood in the doorway and watched and cried his heart out. When she tried to coax him outdoors he cried louder. Time and again I carried him to the garden, and he just stood and cried and shivered, too scared to stay and too scared to run back all that great ten feet to the house.

This continued until one day a dog raced across the garden and snatched Pickle up by the scruff of the neck, dragging him wailing down to the swamp. The Missus and I searched every-where and couldn't find him. Hours later Pickle slunk into the house and hid.

The next morning he went out of his own accord for the first time, settled himself in the middle of the road and dared the dogs to come on. The first dog to come down the road got a walloping it probably remembers to this day. And Pickle wasn't crazy any more.

The odd thing about Pickle's recovery is that the characteristics which were missing during his "breakdown" are predominant in him now. When he stopped being afraid of everything he was afraid of nothing. The world which so terrified him then is now a grab bag crammed full of adventure. He has more curiosity about things which are none of his business than any cat I have ever known.

LANGUAGE

Cats are more successful in making their wishes known to us than we are at communicating with them. Cats' lives aren't cluttered up with words, as ours are, and cats have made panto-mime an art which anyone with eyes can comprehend. The twitch of a whisker expresses pure disdain. There's a world of affection in the gentle wave of a tail. A cat humped for battle is one of the most ferocious sights we can look on. Watch a cat for just one day and you'll realize the clumsy inadequacy of our endless jabbering.

Except in love, anger, and kitten raising, cats very seldom use sound to communicate with each other. I never heard a cat say "Miaou" to another cat, and I believe miaous were invented by cats to help us understand them.

Cats vary in talkativeness as they do in every other way under the sun. Charlie, for example, speaks only when pantomime fails. His gestures are restrained, with a touch of poesy, and they are wonderfully descriptive. Pickle is the talkingest cat I ever knew, and he dramatizes everything. The Missus mugs like the heroine of a silent movie. If mugging fails she shouts as loud as an American talking to a foreigner.

Charlie is the cleverest mime of them all, and so he needs few words. He says "Peep," when he wants in and "Peep," when he wants out and "Peep," when he's hungry. He makes odd little chirruping chuckles to kittens. Even in battle his voice is so small he sounds as if he didn't mean it, which gives him a terrific advantage over loud-mouthed tomcats who are always dismayed when he goes after them like chain lightning.

Ma's vocabulary is simple and explicit, a sort of Basic Cat. Her whole attitude seems to indicate that while people are richer than cats and have a wide superficial knowledge of things which don't concern cats, they are not too bright and must be addressed in the plainest terms.

When she's hungry Ma says "Now!" and she means *now,* not simply miaou. When she's mad at me she says "Wow!" A very gentle "Wow!" means her nose is running and please wipe it, or her head aches and please rub it. When she wants out she says "Miaou." When she wants in she says "Miaou" politely, just once; after that she raises cain. When I come home she greets me with a soft welcoming "Mew." The "Mew" is still softer when in passing I pause to pat her head. When she is supremely happy and would like to share her contentment, Ma rolls and coos delightfully. The coos were a lullaby when she had kittens. In the days when she went hunting, Ma announced her catches with a peculiar, triumphant cry unlike any other sound I ever heard. In love and war she is terrific, simply out of the alphabet.

Pickle has a large vocabulary and talks all the time, having learned when he was young that people are unobservant and slow to comprehend.

When Pickle is hungry he says "Pee-weep," in a plaintive, small voice. If that doesn't fetch food he gets between my feet and trips me. He says "Miaou" when he wants out and in. If left out longer than he considers proper, Pickle's "miaous" develop a desperate quality that makes people ask what ails that cat. His welcome is a low-voiced "Purrrau," saved for special friends.

When Pickle feels like it, we have long conversations about the state of the world. I tell him what I think of the human race, and he says "Purrrr." I ask what he thinks and Pickle says, "Auuu-rrrup." This sometimes goes on for hours, indecisive and in some undefinable way satisfying.

Pickle knows right from wrong, but, being a cat, he does as he pleases, and I scold him. After a severe scolding he jumps on a chair or a table, faces me and chatters like an irate ape. Then he goes back and does wrong again, defiantly.

Both Pickle and Ben imitate birds. Pickle has had lectures on the sacredness of our feathered friends, so he doesn't catch birds. This restraint does not make him like birds. A mockingbird that used to live in our garden pestered Pickle to distraction by coming down a cat's jump and a whisker ahead of him, then flipping into a tree and miaouing or mimicking my whistle. Finally Pickle crouched, cupped his mouth and cheeped like a baby bird. After that they cheeped at each other.

Ben, who hasn't been taught that birds are sacred, makes a similar sound, apparently in the hope of luring a bird near enough to catch it. I have heard of other cats that did this.

Once Pickle barked. A cat-killing dog lumbered onto Pickle's own porch and barked at Pickle through his own screen door.

Pickle hunched himself into a monster of fury and growled. The dog continued to bark. Pickle spat like a locomotive letting off steam. The dog went on barking. Pickle advanced one stiff-legged step, bristled his utmost, and said, "Ah-ah-ah-ah!" in a tight-throated, shrill, unmistakable imitation-bark. The dog hesitated, backed a step. Pickle barked again. The dog drooped off the porch and didn't come back. We who heard this still feel startled when we remember it.

MEMORY AND ANTICIPATION

Cats have excellent memories, when it pleases them. They remember their friends over the years. They remember loved places and the tricks they used to know.

They do not and will not remember anything they'd rather forget. For more than seven years I have been trying to make Pickle remember that the last time he jumped on a table he got spanked, and we're both exactly where we were seven years ago.

Pickle remembers his one long journey, though. At sight of the cat carrier that used to be his, he runs away and hides, and he hasn't been in it for five years. This is memory, not claustrophobia, because Pickle dearly loves to creep into boxes and closets and other hidey-holes.

The Missus remembers her whole life. I know because I saw her relive it. One evening she was sitting on the hood of the car and decided to scratch her ear. She slipped, fell and landed head first on the bumper. She was unconscious for a few minutes and when she came to she had concussion. She couldn't walk straight; her eyes didn't focus and her eyeballs shuddered from side to side appallingly. During the next two hours she lived her life again. In pitiful, quivering pantomime she suckled her mamma and played little kitten games. She ate imaginary food and drank imaginary water. She watched mouse holes and caught phantom mice. She fought and loved, bore kittens, nursed and reared them. I never saw anything like it before, and I hope I never do again.

Cats anticipate events which concern them. All the cats I know that live with working people watch for their folks at home-coming time, though they doze the rest of the day away. Ma, Pickle, and Charlie anticipate bedtime and settle down in their sleeping places about half an hour before the lights go out. Just don't expect the cat to write letters to Santa Claus or remember your birthday.

TEAMWORK

We could take lessons in teamwork from cats. Of all the creatures I know cats are most willing to co-operate with each other, with people, and with any animals they like—provided the co-operation is on an equal basis.

I used to know a black-and-white cat that lived with a white-and-black fox terrier, and they had kittens and puppies about the same time. When either of them tired of the cares of motherhood, she carried her offspring to the other and gallivanted off for an hour or a day or a night, knowing the young ones were well tended.

One little cat I lived with always had her kittens in the car, and as soon as they were born took them to her favorite dog, and they raised the kittens together in the back of his dog house.

All of the cats I have lived with in the country went for walks with me quite as a matter of course, turning aside now and then for a field mouse or a rabbit or a squirrel, not stopping to hunt, just marking the spot I guess, and then continuing the stroll.

When the dog dragged Pickle down to the swamp, I called

Ma to help me find him. She came at once and went ahead of me along the path the dog had taken. We searched together as equals until we lost the trail in the marsh.

Ma, Pickle, and Charlie can rout any enemy. If a large antagonistic dog appears (they don't bother with little dogs) they encircle it, and no matter which way the poor beast turns there's a cat. The dog invariably leaves without a fight.

I watched them dispose of the neighborhood bully, a huge tabby cat that invaded our garden. When I looked out he was in the center of the garden, wishing himself elsewhere. Ma was in front of him, growling and spitting her fiercest (Ma hasn't got tooth-and-claw strength nowadays to daunt a kitten, but she's lionhearted still). Pickle was growling and advancing slowly from the house. Charlie was on the fence doing nothing. The tabby humped his back and bristled defensively while he looked around with the long deliberation of a cat in trouble. Very slowly he began a dragging, sidewise retreat, step by slinking step.

They let him go about six feet, and the Missus rushed him. He scrabbled onto the fence, and there was Charlie, not spitting or growling, not blinking either, just facing him. Pickle sprang to the side fence. The Missus continued to hold the yard. The tabby laid his ears back and inched toward Charlie; Charlie didn't move. The tabby wriggled closer and closer, flexed its legs as if intending to jump over Charlie and keep going. It stood up—and slap, slap, slap! Charlie let him have it right in the snoot. The tabby looked wildly around. Pickle was closing in from behind. The Missus still held our yard. He scrammed.

The people in the apartment house down the block are thinking of erecting a statue, or anyhow planting a catnip bed, in honor of Pickle and Charlie. It seems the place was overrun with rats so bold they went into people's kitchens and bit them.

Then the cats and I moved into the block, and Pickle and Charlie went to work. According to the tenants there, Charlie arrives first and stations himself in a corner of the inner area-way. Pickle comes and takes the opposite corner. They wait until a rat comes out. If it's nearer to Pickle he gets it. If it's on Charlie's side it's his. If one cat jumps and misses, the other closes in. Once Charlie caught a rat insecurely and it tore loose, turned and attacked him. Pickle got it in mid-leap. The boys used to catch a daily quota of five or six rats, while the neighbors cheered. Now I'm told there aren't any rats.

HUMOR

All of the higher animals, including man, have some sense of humor. Animal humor is usually of the custard-pie variety, and for that reason may be overlooked by people, who invented custard pies.

Cat humor is mostly slapstick, but a cat is never a clown. The joke is always on the other fellow. When a cat shows off it expects to be admired, not laughed at. Ma loves to wear bows, the bigger the better, and she struts absurdly in a flowered doll's hat—so long as no one laughs at her. At the first snicker she rips her finery off and struts away with the same backward kick of a hind foot that is her answer to the indignity of a spanking.

Her notion of humor is to lurk under a table or chair until an unsuspecting cat passes by, give it a hearty smack on the bottom, and duck. The other cat is always insulted and usually beats her up. She doesn't mind the beating—she's had her fun.

Pickle and Charlie do the same thing, and dearly love to pounce out at people and then scamper off; but this has more of the elements of a game than of humor. Charlie plays more

The practical joke

than any of the cats, but I don't think I ever saw him do anything that could be classed definitely as humor. His play is tender and sweet, with a touch of fantasy.

When Ben used to fetch Oscar the frog home in the dead of night and turn it loose to leap moistly in and out of people's beds, he seemed to be having a whale of a time. His people didn't enjoy the joke until after they had prevailed on the frog's owner to take her pet up to Central Park and turn it loose. On the other hand, we are often amused by animal doings that aren't funny to them. When Ben brings home a mouse with trap attached, I think he's merely doing the best he can and feels apologetic about the mouse trap.

I don't know whether Pickle drags his dead snakes in the house and coils them neatly on rugs because he thinks dead snakes are funny, or because he wants to brag. Dead snakes amuse me only in retrospect, and some of Pickle's humor is even harder to enjoy. One morning I awoke to find my best nightgown spread out on the floor. Under it there was a great mound of shredded newspaper. Under the confetti, on a whole paper, there was a large dead rat. Pickle sat by and watched me disinter the rat with all the smug pride of a successful practical joker, which I think he was.

THE GOLDEN RULE

We preach the Golden Rule and practice it when convenient. The people who do unto others more than they could possibly expect others to do for them, or give without any thought of recompense, are saints to some of us and suckers to the rest. Somehow we never take them for granted. Selfishness and indifference seem to be normal, saints and sinners notable. It's just as well that cats don't know about this—if they did they'd probably pick up and leave us, for cats abide by the Golden Rule somewhat better than we do.

The cats that have adopted other cats' kittens, puppies, squirrels, rabbits and even rats, are past counting. Cynical people claim that these strange babies are adopted merely to use the cat's surplus milk. Without bothering to answer that, I'll point to the cats, almost as numerous, who adopt baby chickens and ducks and other little birds in need of cuddling. Birds don't suckle.

The ability of cats to get along with other animals, and their considerateness toward strange creatures, continued to surprise me for a long time. Spattie taught me to accept the goodheartedness of cats as part of their nature.

Spattie was a dumb little puss, but she had her points. She lived with a macaw, a monkey, a little blind canary, and the fish that bit her tongue. The macaw and the monkey raised her, and she seemed to regard them as her parents rather than two oddly assorted creatures. When Spattie had a guilty conscience she'd go to the monkey for protection—and she got it! When she'd been caught in the act and punished, she'd go to the macaw for consolation, and Mac would spread his bright wing across her shoulders and smooth her fur and gurgle sympathetically. Spattie took her cat naps curled around the blind canary's necessarily very small cage. He seemed to like having her there. He'd sit close to her on chilly days and when he felt gay, which was surprisingly often, he'd peck at her fur and preen her whiskers. When Spattie grew up and caught mice she brought them to the monkey. She'd lay a dead mouse at its feet, purring proudly, and the monkey would leap for the ceiling, scared out of her wits but too fond of her kitten to punish it.

I used to know a green parrot and a cat that lived together and were great friends. When the parrot in a moment of exuberance chewed through a lamp cord and almost electrocuted itself, the cat pulled the parrot away and began licking its back, which was exactly the right thing to do, though of course the cat couldn't have known that. At first their people thought the cat was hurting the parrot and tried to separate them. The cat refused to leave and they realized it was trying to help its friend.

Charlie is the helpful one at our house. Once he came to me in a great state of agitation, pawing at me and tossing his head toward the windows. Following him, I found a sick pigeon huddled in the corner of the sill. Charlie chirruped sympathetically and began to lick the pigeon's feathers. An unidentified lunatic was poisoning pigeons at the time, so I took Charlie in for fear he'd be poisoned, and prepared to telephone the S.P.C.A. In the interval the pigeon flew away. It was plain that Charlie had no intention of eating the pigeon. Don't forget it was Charlie who found the Joes and brought them home.

Charlie always looks out for his friends. While I was working on this book Charlie came to me and pawed at my arm, jumped in my lap, sat on the typewriter and bumped his face against mine. Charlie never bothers me when I'm working, so I said, "What is it, Charles?" He jumped down and ran to the back windows, hopped on a sill and began to call anxiously. Pickle was sitting in the yard with his head down. I thought he'd brought a rat home from the apartment house and was watching it. I said, "Don't be jealous, Charlie—go get a rat of your own." Charlie sailed out into the yard and began to lick Pickle's head, calling to me all the time. I spoke to Pickle and he didn't move, so I hurried out. Poor Pickle's face had been bashed in and he was totally blinded by blood. Some unspeakable devil had hit him in the face with a coal shovel. If Charlie hadn't told me, Pickle might have died of strangulation because his nose was crushed right into his head. Pickle is well now, though he lost all of his front teeth and seems to have a trace of sinus trouble. Actually, he's handsomer than he was because his nose is shorter and twice as broad, both points of beauty in cats, but I'd rather have had him unchanged.

No matter what we do to them, cats continue to love us and do their little best to help us in time of need. Gordon Stables, in *The Domestic Cat,* tells an authentic story of a ploughman who was ill and too poor to buy the meat his doctor prescribed. All that saved him was his cat, which brought in a rabbit or a bird every day. Stables also tells about a young cat that lost a leg in a trap, and while it was recovering from the injury an old cat on the place brought birds, mice, and sympathy. Agnes Repplier—*The Fireside Sphinx*—knew a cat that fetched game every day to the woman it lived with. Poor people in the South quite often teach their cats to fetch in rabbits and squirrels. This, of course, is poaching, and may shock fanatical conservationists. Normal people consider the spirit of the giver.

Josephine, the female one of Charlie's Joes, paid board. When she was still a small kitten Josephine began bringing me presents. Since she had access only to the inner part of a city block, Josephine's gifts were limited in character and could not possibly have pleased anything except another half-starved cat. Every evening about dinnertime, occasionally during dinner, Josephine dragged in a mouse, a chewed-up rat, or a rabbit's foot scavenged from a neighborhood restaurant and presented it to me. Unpleasant and ill timed as these gifts were, they were the offerings of a forlorn little creature who had been abandoned by one human family and was, at best, tolerated at my house. Josephine was always hungry and she could have eaten those things where she found them instead of contributing her kitten's mite.

Since Ma stopped raising kittens she has brought all her

catches to me, and if I'm low in my mind she comforts me. She climbs in my lap and rolls and purrs and blows down my neck. Once when I was very sad she licked the skin off my cheek while trying to comfort me.

She comforts Pickle and Charlie if they're ailing, and last year they took turns nursing her. The Missus was very ill and had agonizing headaches which seemed to be relieved only when another cat licked her head. Pickle and Charlie and the Joes licked in shifts, night and day, for more than a week. I think they saved her life.

When I'm ill the cats smother me with attention. Pickle sits on my chest and purrs loudly. The Missus licks the skin off me. Charlie strews old bones and dog biscuits all over me. I don't claim that this is salutary, but it does get one out of bed.

Even swarms of cats can abide by the Golden Rule. I can't imagine a tougher cross section of the cat population than the free-lance cats of New York's Greenwich Village, which extends from the ivory towers of Washington Square and Fifth Avenue to the North River docks. Yet they behaved with tolerance and circumspection when the cat-meat-man came around.

During the late twenties the cat-meat-man started out early every evening with a pail in each hand. He went from speakeasy to speakeasy collecting meat scraps for the cats, routing his course so as to arrive at Charles Street and Seventh Avenue when the pails were full. The cats got there before he did. They came from everywhere, frisking, limping, doddering and dragging—bulging mamma cats, mewing kittens and battle-scarred toms, fifty or seventy-five of them every night, all the cats in the Village that nobody cared about except the cat-meat-man. They sat side by side on the stoops, on the street, all over the gas station, alert, silent, waiting.

When the cat-meat-man came into view their ears and

whiskers twitched. Otherwise they didn't move. He went down the line, doling out a chicken wing here, a steak scrap there, a bit of scallopini to the next one, giving something to every cat. They waited their turn, quivering with eagerness, drooling sometimes, and each cat accepted its portion without complaint or comparison, and ate, and went away until the next night.

I watched the cat-meat-man feed them dozens of times and never saw a fight or any jostling. I never saw one starved cat try to steal from another. I've often wondered whether a crowd of humans as hungry as those cats would have been quite so gentlemanly.

Appendix

CATS AND CALENDARS

In China, Siam, and most other oriental countries the cat owns a year of the calendar. Oriental calendars run in large cycles of sixty years and small cycles of twelve years. Each year of the small cycle has an animal name and symbol. In Siam, the first is The Year of the Rat; second, The Year of the Cow; third, The Year of the Tiger; fourth, The Year of the Hare; fifth, The Year of the Big Drake; sixth, The Year of the Small Drake; seventh, The Year of the Cat; eighth, The Year of the Goat; ninth, The Year of the Monkey; tenth, The Year of the Cock; eleventh, The Year of the Dog; twelfth, The Year of the Pig. Young people wishing to marry must choose mates whose year supplements theirs. For example, a young man born in The Year of the Cat may marry a Pig-girl or a Cow-girl, but not a Lion- or Dog-girl.

CATS' EYES

Charles H. Ross, in *The Book of Cats,* says the Chinese tell time by the expanding and contracting pupils of cats' eyes. He adds that if cats could talk they'd tell the Chinese the day of the week as well.

This peculiarity of cats' eyes inspired Occidentals to associate cats with the moon, which waxes and wanes, and therefore with witchcraft, black magic, and other human shenannigans.

The fact that cats' eyes glow in the dark is another complication. The Chinese believe that houses are haunted by spirit cats with great blazing eyes.

DEVIL CATS

Devil cats are very scarce in oriental folklore.

The Japanese believe in Nekomata, a not-very-bad devil cat with a forked tail, which often changes itself into a woman. Geisha girls are sometimes called Neko, cat-tongued, because they are insincere flatterers. The term "cat-eyed" is used to describe a fickle person, and the Japanese equivalent of poker-faced is "cat-faced."

The Chinese, being more intelligent people, don't take much stock in devil cats. Instead they specialize in nice stories about cats that sacrificed their lives to save their people, and cats that expressed lavish appreciation for small favors.

CATS AND THE WEATHER

Cats are recognized the world around as weather prophets, and in some places are gravely consulted on the subject.

In England a hundred and fifty years ago people believed that if the cat turned its tail to the fire there would be a hard frost. If the cat licked its tail rain was due. When puss washed over her left eye a stranger was coming to the house. If the cat sneezed several times in succession everyone in the family would have a cold in the head.

Far away and long ago, you say? Oh, no. When Neville Chamberlain went to Munich anxious crowds stood in front of Number 10 Downing Street day after day, listening for any scrap of news, and arguing earnestly whether good news or bad was presaged when Joey, the Chamberlain's black cat, washed his right ear. Some insisted that the cleanliness of Joey's right ear could affect only the weather, while others held that it influenced the state of the world.

Sailors believe that when a cat suddenly begins to frolic, a gale is coming. For proof they point to the little ripplings seen on the sea during the dead calm that precedes a storm—those ripples aren't called "cat's paws" for nothing, they're caused by ghost cats dancing ahead of bad weather. We perpetuate this myth when we say of a frisking cat that "It has the wind up its tail."

In the Harz Mountains of Germany the stormy northwest wind is still called "the cat's nose."

Before cats came to Europe the wolf and the dog symbolized big and little winds. When cats arrived they were put in charge of rain. To this day we describe a heavy, windy rain by saying it's raining cats and dogs.

Cats do face in the direction from which the wind blows—if they can't by any manner of means get out of the wind. They do this to avoid being chilled when their fur is blown the wrong way. So far as I know, all other animals and birds have the same habit for the same reason.

In Lapland, where life and death often depend on weather, the family cat is always consulted before a journey is undertaken. Black cats are believed to be reincarnated relatives, and their advice is sought on the most important matters.

The Japanese and Chinese also believe that black cats can foretell the weather.

Sailors everywhere consider tortoise-shell cats lucky. Asiatic seamen pay fabulous prices for them because pied cats know earlier than any others when a storm is coming and climb to the top of the tallest mast to charm away the storm devils. Images of cats are used as a last resort, though the sailors know they're not the real McCoy. The ship that bore the holy Buddha texts from China to Japan was guarded by a golden cat.

NAMES AND NICKNAMES

The dog is known by a thousand names, the cat by three. Cats every place in the world answer to *cat, pussy,* or *miaou.*

The ancient Egyptians called the cat *mau.* The Chinese call the cat *mao.*

From North Africa to Norway a cat is a cat. It may be written *gado,* as in Africa; *gato* as in Spain; *chat* as in France, or *cat* or *kat*—the word is the same. Our *kitty* comes from the Turkish *kedi,* and it's still cat.

In Java, Indonesia, and like places, the cat is *bus, busi, pus* or *pusa,* so if you call, "Pussy, pussy," east of Suez and south of China the cats will understand. In Switzerland, also, Pussy is called *busi.*

In France and Belgium a cat is spoken of as "un chat," but it is addressed as "Minou," the way we say "Puss."

In England, before the Crusaders learned "Kitty, kitty," from the Turks, a kitten was called a *catling.* A tomcat was always a tom, and female cats used to be called *Moll* or *Malkin,* as when the cat mews in "Macbeth," and the witch calls, "I come, Gray-malkin."

The word *cat* probably has more diversified meanings than any other in our language. *Cat* is a cat and a whip and a ship and most of the parts of a ship. *Cat* is a tripod with the legs crossed in the middle, simply and aptly named because no matter how you drop it, it lights on its feet. And *cat* is a gossiping woman.

In Scotland, as I said before, *cat* is a cat, *cat* is war, and *cat* is a fighting man. Warriors are *catti. Cateran* means a band of fighting men of a highland clan. *Catu rigis* are little kings. County Caithness is the Cat County, and Sutherland, which once was part of Caithness, is *Catur* in Gaelic. *A'caithris* means a watch by night—the cat watch. *Cait* is the genitive singular of cat, and it also means lascivious desire for the opposite sex, as, "Deedy caits after yon lass like a lovesick cat."

Then we have "A cat in the meal"—a hidden danger. "Cat and dog life," "Enough to make a cat laugh," "Wait and see which way the cat jumps," "To let the cat out of the bag," the games of tip-cat and one-old-cat, "Sick as a cat" and the nine lives of a cat. There's the cat's cradle and the cat's paw, catnaps and catcalls and caterwauling, catnip and cattails and catfish, pussywillows and catkins. Caterpillar comes from *Catus pilosus,* the cat-haired. We have cat-birds and cat-haws and the jewel, cat's eye, a cat-stitch in embroidery and catgut, which is made from the intestines of sheep, preferably undernourished sheep, and not from cats' guts at all.

We all grew up knowing the nonsense of "Ding, dong dell, Pussy in the well" and "Hey, diddle, diddle, the cat and the fiddle," "Three little kittens lost their mittens," "Pussy cat, Pussy cat, where have you been?" and "The gingham dog and the calico cat."

When as a child I grew out of the "What's that?" stage into the "What's that for?" stage, all foolish or repetitious questions were answered with, "Cat's fur to make kitten breeches," and I was often told that "Curiosity killed the cat."

We say, "All cats look alike in the dark," or "At night all cats are gray." The Chinese say, "The cat does not catch mice for God," and "If you would be friends with the cat on Tuesday, don't kick it on Monday."

Dick Whittington's cat, they say, was a cat boat built in the Norwegian style, narrow in the stern with projecting quarters and a deep waist, and Dick grew rich by carrying coals from

Newcastle to London. Coal was first shipped commercially from Newcastle to London in 1381, and Dick became Lord Mayor in 1397, so it's all very likely, I'm sorry to say.

The grin of the Cheshire Cat was created in Cheshire cheese, which always used to be moulded in the shape of a laughing cat's head.

The tale of the Kilkenny cats is an allegory. The two cats that fought in the sawpit until nothing was left but their tails represent the towns of Kilkenny and Irishtown whose inhabitants battled until the end of the Seventeenth Century over their boundaries and their rights, and at the finish only two tails of debt were left.

"What a long tail our cat's got," demonstrates the amazing endurance of an apt colloquialism. Long, long ago an English lad who'd taken a very short voyage came home so full of the wonder of far places that he pretended to have forgotten all the home things. The climax came when he asked his mother what she called "that long-tailed beggar." She told him that was old Puss, the cat. He shook his head wonderingly and said, "My, what a long tail our cat's got!" and he hasn't lived it down yet.

LEGENDS

Before the flood, the god of the Buriats told his chosen man that high water was coming and advised him to build a ship in the forest, instructing him not to tell anyone what he was doing. The man told his wife and that opened the way for the Buriat devil, who stowed away, disguised as a rat, when the animals came aboard. They were no sooner afloat than the devil began to gnaw holes in the ship and it seemed that they must sink. The woman, who wasn't to blame for her husband's indiscretion, prayed with all her might, and the Buriat god sent a cat to catch the rat devil.

The Chinese believe that the first cat was the offspring of a monkey and a lioness, which isn't very original of them because they attribute the same beginning to the Pekingese dog. This miraculous origin doesn't prevent the Chinese from fattening cats and eating them, nor from selling cat skins to the cat-fur-man when he comes around.

When Buddha died all the animals congregated and sat in respectful silence, mourning him. Only the rat, forever greedy, took advantage of this and began to lap the oil in the lamp. The cat dutifully killed the rat. Because this murder, however necessary, was disrespectful under the circumstances, the cat sacrificed its rightful place in the Zodiac.

An old Palestinian legend has it that once upon a time a duty was assigned to each and every animal on earth, except the cat and dog who were excused from work because of their respective virtues of cleanliness and fidelity. A written document was given to them, which they could show if anyone tried to make them work. The dog took charge of it and buried it with his old bones. The horse and the ox were jealous because they too had virtues and had not been given a dispensation, so they bribed the rat to burrow and destroy the diploma. Since then the dog has been chained for his carelessness and the cat has never forgiven him.

According to the Turks, this is why the cat washes after dinner: Long, long ago a cat caught a sparrow. The sparrow fluttered and said, "Oh, you dirty cat, don't you know you should wash before dinner!" The cat, which prided itself on its cleanliness, promptly began to wash, and the sparrow flew away. One lesson was enough, and ever since that day cats have washed after dinner.

Ages and ages ago, on an island in the Pacific Ocean, a beautiful white cat lived who gave birth to a girl child. The cat loved her girl child very much and took good care of her. They were both sweet and gentle and loving, so when their time on earth was done they were wafted up to the moon. If you go to the Oceanic Islands and gaze long at the moon when it is full, you can see them there, rocking in the sky.

Index